Cycles in the UK Housing Economy

David Gray

Cycles in the UK Housing Economy

Price and its Relationship with Lenders, Buyers, Consumption and Construction

palgrave
macmillan

David Gray
Lincoln University
Lincoln, UK

ISBN 978-3-319-63347-3 ISBN 978-3-319-63348-0 (eBook)
DOI 10.1007/978-3-319-63348-0

Library of Congress Control Number: 2017948263

Printed on acid-free paper

This Palgrave Macmillan imprint is published by Springer Nature
The registered company is Springer International Publishing AG
The registered company address is: Gewerbestrasse 11, 6330 Cham, Switzerland

Contents

List of Figures

List of Tables

1

Introduction

Abstract The introduction covers the issues to be raised and the data and methods utilised. The propositions, in no particular order, are as follows:

- The cycles found in economic series are stable.
- There is greater volatility in repeat buyers/more expensive/better quality housing markets.
- New housing should be distinguishable from second hand. It should be less volatile than second-hand property prices.
- There should be a stronger link between house prices and consumption expenditure in the liberalised era.
- Price diffusion across space could be explained by imbalanced economy urban system models or by balance economy/polycentric models. Which is the more representative is an empirical issue.

Keywords Price diffusion · House cycles · Housing economies
Housing market

D. Gray, *Cycles in the UK Housing Economy*,
DOI 10.1007/978-3-319-63348-0_1

1.1 Housing Economics: The Macro, Micro, and Meso Levels of Analysis

Housing markets are not analysed by traditional pricing theory easily. One can highlight a series of complicating factors.

- Houses have both consumption and investment dimensions (Dusansky and Wilson 1993). As such, they can be viewed as assets that return a financial yield as well as utility. Moreover, a dwelling is durable, such that it can be consumed for a lifetime and then sold on as something still habitable.
- Dwellings commonly are priced at a multiple of most people's annual income, so that most owners can only afford to own one home at a time. Under these circumstances, the notion of consuming greater volume with rising income does not apply. However, more housing services can be consumed in terms of housing characteristics. This can be seen in a pattern of purchases over time. The first dwelling purchase may not have the desired properties or that housing preferences change with stages of a life cycle. For many over a lifetime, there is serial home ownership. Indeed, preferences may alter, not only with age but also with personal circumstances. Dwelling house families in the majority, not individuals, whose needs change with the age profile of the family unit.
- The majority of house purchasers in the UK are capital constrained, turning to mortgage providers to fund at least one of their house purchases. This means that both a borrower and lender would/should have some notion of the limits of affordability. Thus, there is a joint decision over the purchase agreement.
- Housing in the UK comprises mostly second-hand dwellings. Although at any one time the market will comprise new and second hand in more equal proportions, in the absence of a developed insurance market for purchases, there is a significant agency problem. Second-hand houses commonly are bought as seen.
- The essential nature of a dwelling is to provide shelter. Given that its location is unique and it is spatially immobile, the dwelling's

proximity to amenities and places of employment is key to its desirability and central to some form of price modelling.

- Although some are sold at auction (in Scotland), commonly there is a bilateral trade between a pair of buyers and sellers. One could see the housing market price less akin to a Walrasian auction and more like a search and matching process.
- Dwellings in a locale may be not too dissimilar at the outset but they evolve with time. An extension could be added. Also, they depreciate. As such, they are heterogeneous nature. Moreover, buyers' valuations are not homogenous. Characteristics, such as original features, will command a premium with some buyers.
- Dwelling ownership entails carrying costs. These reoccurring costs would include interest and most likely capital payments on the mortgage, expenses maintaining the property, and property taxes. It is not clear that all buyers recognise these costs when purchasing a dwelling supported by this mortgage.
- There are high agency costs for the lender. The agency problem arises for the lender over the unobserved financial rectitude of the borrower. Asymmetric information can be reduced by seeking evidence of 'financial good character', but this disfavours those with poor credit histories or little exposure to the credit market. Alternatively, the smaller mortgage might be proffered by the lender, forcing the borrower to find a greater down payment.
- The offer price is a signal to the market about the quality of the stated characteristics in the brochure. Given an asymmetry of information and consequent moral hazard on the part of the vendor with the adverse selection possible, the rational buyer would investigate further the characteristics of the dwelling. To the potential buyer, getting to the point of making an offer is costly. Legal searches, structural surveys, and the like need to satisfy both the buyer and the buyer's mortgage provider that the dwelling is not overpriced.
- As an asset, the ownership of a dwelling forms part of the owner's wealth and as such their consumption expenditure and savings activity. As it displaces other sacrifices, a rise in property value could reduce the latter and raise the former. The pursuit of a dwelling should generate the opposite reaction, boosting savings and lowering

consumption. One could see a life-cycle dimension to these propositions. Those seeking to join the housing market could be sacrificing consumption today for property ownership tomorrow.

- A capital constraint, restricting an owner to one 'affordable' house at any one time, poses problems when selling. The house seller could also be a house buyer themselves, and so a party to two dependent trades. The seller may require a buyer to relieve them of their existing house whilst providing some of the finance for the purchase of their own purchase. The house they want to buy should be free so that they can move in. So, there can be a *chain* of sales/purchases concluded on a single day.
- Rising prices favour the equity or wealth of the repeat buyer/current dwelling owner (hereon recognised as RB). This injects greater purchasing power into the hands of an owner–buyer, adding price volatility to the marketplace. The speculative nature of some sellers will inject further volatility: they can join the market with little time or cost constraints, adding turnover volatility when prices are already accelerating or leave when prices are not buoyant.
- The other buyer group of note, the first-time buyer (FTB), comes to the market with non-housing equity. As they are priced out rather than in a property upturn, the FTB fits the standard theoretical consumer model. Their market participation will depend on income and credit and, by implication, changes in credit rationing.
- As the quality of the dwelling could be changing over time, the mix of housing that is marketed could vary from year to year. To cater for this, price index providers, such as the Nationwide, make adjustments for the quality mix variation.

Given these impediments how might one analyse the housing market?

Gibb (2009) proffers a spirited defence of the use of mainstream economic theory in the face of calls for a more interdisciplinary approach. DiPasquale and Wheaton (1996) propose that housing economics draws its theoretical grounding from both macro- and microeconomics. In microeconomics, the focus of attention is the behaviour of the representative individual, firm or sector. Macroeconomics focuses on the spaceless world of aggregate measures of activity, such as total or average income, unemployment, and inflation. In between are regional and urban economics. The former has had a spatial macroeconomics flavour where the use of aggregates subdivided by spatial areas, such as regions, is studied. Regions are sometimes modelled as small open economies that trade with the outside world. Measures, such as exports, are important. Indeed, there is a strong relationship between regional and international economics, where regions can be viewed as in countries an international trading system but without the added complication of a currency.

Urban economics, by contrast, can trace much of its heritage to microeconomics. Marginal analysis of land-use and rents, location and transport costs are featured (Vickerman 1984). However, even cities are sometimes modelled as small open economies (e.g. Bogart 1998). By their very nature, as they are immobile, buildings have a spatial dimension. If all spatial units were fractals or perfect miniature replicas of the nation, they are necessarily homogeneous, negating the rationale for a sub-national economic or portfolio consideration; sub-economies would behave identically. At the other extreme, if all spatial units were unique, no general statement could be formulated about any set, and the whole would be a weighted average of its subsets. At the meso level, subdividing a larger unit, like a nation, into (super-) regions, would require homogeneity internally but heterogeneity inter-regionally. Practically speaking, internal differences should be less than external distinctions.

DiPasquale and Wheaton (1996) point out that the distinction between micro- and macroeconomics in real estate analysis is in the approach to define the market. In a micro sense, a market requires homogeneity. As houses are unique, spatially this is problematic. Moreover, dwellings come in a number of forms, such as terraced semi-detached and detached houses; flats; number of floors; number of bedrooms; and garage/garden. As such, the notion of a homogeneous market is hopeful. Some studies mitigate this problem by analysing data from sales of the same properties over time. It is not uncommon to see a recently completed housing estate of 20 houses to find that they are built in a common style, they would have broadly the same access to amenities, but the number of bedrooms varies. A value could be imputed for the marginal bedroom.

One concern for this sub-market description is that in the eyes of buyers, a two bedroom flat may be a close substitute for two bedroomed terraced, semi-detached, or detached houses. Moreover, four bedrooms and five bedrooms detached may not be all that different to a buyer. For Pryce and Evans (2007), significantly different price trajectories of a homogeneous housing unit are indicative of local or sub-markets, but this is micro modelling. DiPasquale and Wheaton (1996) argue that despite being different, they are not necessarily distinct if the different properties react in a similar manner to macro factors.

Land as a commodity is almost fixed in supply and so is almost perfectly price inelastic. Its availability underpins only the general level of house prices (DiPasquale and Wheaton 1996). By contrast, land use and relative values of land vary with location. Land has a number of competing uses: agriculture, housing, retail outlets, commercial, or industrial use.

With land and property, restrictions that permit normal supply and demand analysis to be used are not fulfilled, so alternative approaches to property analyses have developed. One approach, adopted by authors such as DiPasquale and Wheaton, is based on compensating differentials. The owner of the land is compensated for inconvenience in one dimension or element of their utility function by lower price in another. The market involves at least two elements that are traded-off. For example, when modelling land use and rents, a key approach to accommodation revolves around the disutility of commuting to the place of work. The greater the disutility felt by an individual or a group, the greater their desire to live closer to their place of employment *ceteris paribus*. Greater demand for accommodation closer to a centre of employment inflates rents nearer to the centre compared with places further away. Thus, paying higher rent is compensated by lower commuting costs. This is an equilibrium approach that is predicated on a swift adjustment process to deviations from those differentials.

Even though houses may be distinct in location and type, house prices could maintain stable differentials. An increase in demand for one type of housing, through close substitutability, boosts the demand of others, pushing up the price of all housing in the local area. This could occur relatively swiftly.

The same process, though, could occur through overspill. As some locals look further afield to a neighbouring area that too would experience an increase in demand, boosting prices. The spillover between areas will be slower than within locales.

As an existing homeowner requires a buyer for their house to provide some of the resources for the purchase of the next one, it is likely that the housing 'chain' of buyers and sellers requires someone to be joining, property free. The lifeblood of the housing market is the first-time buyer. As a guide, people trade-up, buying larger houses as their income and personal circumstances dictate. At the end of their working or independent lives, people trade-down or move into shared or sheltered accommodation. Thus, first-time buyers join a conveyor belt when they are young, moving up the property ladder, leaving or trading down when their large house becomes unmanageable or too expensive to run.

Banks and building societies should be prudent. Like other financial institutions, public faith in what they do is essential. They should not lend money on an irresponsible basis; the borrower should be able to repay the loan. However, they make money on making loans and that means they have a vested interest in maintaining a healthy rate of house purchases. This imperative encourages them to expand their market by offering incentives to potential mortgagees, such as discounted mortgages. Sometimes these financial incentives lead to inappropriate behaviour. The traditional method of assessing affordability is the price-earnings ratio. Historically, the UK average 'multiple' is around 3.1–3.25. It has been argued that banks and building societies may drift from long-run income house price multiples if they believe that the expected increases in house prices will overcome any costs of default and housing reclamation. Minsky, among others, believes that this drift is cyclical and potentially financially problematic.

1.2 The Scope of the Work

This work examines the interaction between UK and regional house price cycles and some associated macroeconomics variables, using, in the main, spectral analysis. DiPasquale and Wheaton (1996) aver that the supply of land sets the overall market price level but it is a demand that determines relative property values, and it is here that attention should be focused when seeking to examine why the prices of land and property vary considerably within the same locale or market. Although affordability is commonly assessed on the basis of current income, DiPasquale and Wheaton report that permanent income is a better predictor of housing consumption. Housing and other forms of consumption are both substitutes and complement over differing time horizons. The relaxation of credit restrictions should see co-movement of both. However, it is posited that the pursuit of one at an early stage in the life cycle would lead to a reduction of the other. Consumption is further divided into consumer durables and non-durables, with financing also subdivided into secured and unsecured lending. One would expect non-durables would be less cyclically sensitive compared with durables. Lending though could be either pro-cyclical reflecting relaxed credit constraints or counter-cyclical reflecting strained personal balance sheets.

Various threads of house price diffusion literature are considered. The first, the ripple effect, entails house price diffusion across space. The most discussed field is where regional house price increases in the UK appear to be led by London and the South East (*inter alia* Meen 1999; Gray 2012). The novel contribution to this field is the application of buyer types.

The second thread entails price diffusion among housing of differing quality tiers (Coulson and McMillen 2007; Ho et al. 2008; Hui 2011; Smith and Ho 1996). Building on a model due to Stein (1995), Mayer (1993) argues it is not necessarily quality but price that matters: high-priced homes are sensitive to low-priced ones. Within this group, one can place a field where first-time buyers and repeat buyers are arranged in a rank order or a ladder. Here, authors such as Ortalo-Magné and Rady (2006), Sommervoll et al. (2010), and Borgersen (2014a, b, c) see equity transfers between these buyer groups. The higher quality/more expensive houses are subject to greater price volatility.

A third strand entailing considering a ripple through these differing housing vintages if such relationships should be found. Both Gray (2015) and Cook and Holly (2000), consider three housing vintages: *New, Modern,* and *Older* dwellings.

The house price data is drawn from a single source, Nationwide Building Society covering two periods: 1955–2014 and 1983–2014. The second period is just over half the length of the first falling side an era of mortgage market liberalisation that took place during the 1980s. Whereas households had previously been constrained in their access to mortgage credit, from the 1980s, it became much easier to borrow to finance consumers' expenditure, using increased housing wealth as collateral. This corresponds with a period described as the great moderation.

There is a consideration of housing supply in the form of dwelling construction. Given the nature of the analysis, one could consider the sensitivity of construction to dwelling price and vice versa. One would expect that, in the short-run, prices would be mostly demand driven, but over a longer horizon, increased supply would place downward pressure on price.

Rather than a long-run trend to which an economy is drawn, De Groot and Franses (2008) argue that long-term economic stability comes from the persistence of multiple, robust cycles that enable the system to absorb exogenous shocks that would otherwise put mature economies 'off balance'. Overall, they conclude that an economic cycle could be represented by a few frequencies.

1.2.1 What Propositions Are Explored?

In no particular order, there are a number of issues that arise that result from the approach taken, challenging or supporting findings from other authors.

- De Groot and Franses (2008) suggest there are two views on the presence of economic cycles. Recent ideas such as New Classical and New Keynesian business cycle theory, for example, do not even recognise the notion of a periodicity. These models posit that the fluctuations are based on shocks and reaction to shocks. Undulations are caused by shocks that are exogenous and are largely unpredictable and are described here as the *shock* perspective. Mainstream economics conceptualises markets as essentially stable in nature with any shock that causes a deviation (in the short-run) from the long-run steady state as temporary. De Groot and Franses argue that long-term economic stability comes from the persistence of multiple, robust cycles. Mainstream models seek a long-term outcome: cyclical models anticipate persistent periodicities in series.

- Ortalo-Magné and Rady (2006) (OMR), Borgersen (2014a, b), and Sommervoll et al. (2010) propose that the RB and FTB buyers are in separate but hierarchically arranged property markets. The RB group is reliant on the FTB for equity. Moreover, the FTB prices are amplified in RB markets, implying that there is greater volatility in RB/more expensive/better quality housing markets.
- New housing should be distinguishable from second hand. New housing as it was is a first-time sale. New dwellings capture for the builder the capital that would otherwise be transferred from one homeowner to another. As it falls outside of the repeat buyer price acceleration, it should be less volatile than second-hand property prices.
- House prices and consumption should be linked jointly to be consequences of greater financial liberalisation. Moreover, a wealth effect due to rising prices should impact upon consumption. In effect, there should be a stronger link between house prices and consumption expenditure in the liberalised era.
- The impact of globalised/financial liberalised era (the great moderation 1985–2007) could, according to Campbell and Mankiw (1991), allow some free(r) to allocate consumption associated with permanent income. This has implications for the business cycle periodicity. Consumption should be spread over a range of long frequencies.
- Price diffusion across space could be explained by imbalanced economy urban system models or by balance economy/polycentric models. One distinguishing feature in house prices is in the level and extent of regional volatilities. Second is in the order of response. If there is a dominant cycle, one would expect it to feature a London marker. Subsequent price increase should be ordered according to size of the city. A ripple thesis posits distance from London is the key marker.

1.3 Data and Methods of Data Analysis

Two methodologies are employed: the first from recent innovations by Pesaran and the second from spectral analysis. Spectral methods are selected to reflect an overtly cyclical approach to the analysis and to test the Sommervoll et al. (2010) simulation implications. The frequency domain work deals with cycles. The time domain work provides an analysis of trend. Both offer a means of discerning market leadership.

Figure 1.1 displays the Nationwide Building Society housing regions that relate to the data used. Buyer groups, regional data, and vintages all come from this source on a quarterly basis for 32 or 60 years.

1.4 The Structure of the Work

In contributions in the field, which follows, here is a consideration of the notable work that addresses some of the issues raised later on. For example, in keeping with the cycle and balanced and imbalanced economy themes, a body of work featured is of economic integration at the European level and the issue of changes in the degree of co-movement of the cycle component. This is followed by an exposition of Housing Market Theory, featuring DiPasquale and Wheaton's (1996) perspective of the monocentric urban model. This model is useful as it explains common house price movements without common house price levels. This is extended to cover polycentric models and urban systems.

The methods covered in the fourth chapter feature spectral analysis and unit root tests. Rather than testing for cointegration to establish long-term equilibrium, there is a consideration of a pairwise differential relationship. Unit root tests are employed including innovations due to Pesaran (2007). Some of the spectral results are replicated in the time domain to explore whether they support or conflict with those using more conventional techniques. The spectral methods involve the discussion of new measures of cohesion and synchronisation. This is important as asynchronicity is, by definition, a characteristic of a ripple effect. Cycles are extracted using filters, most commonly the Hodrick-Prescott

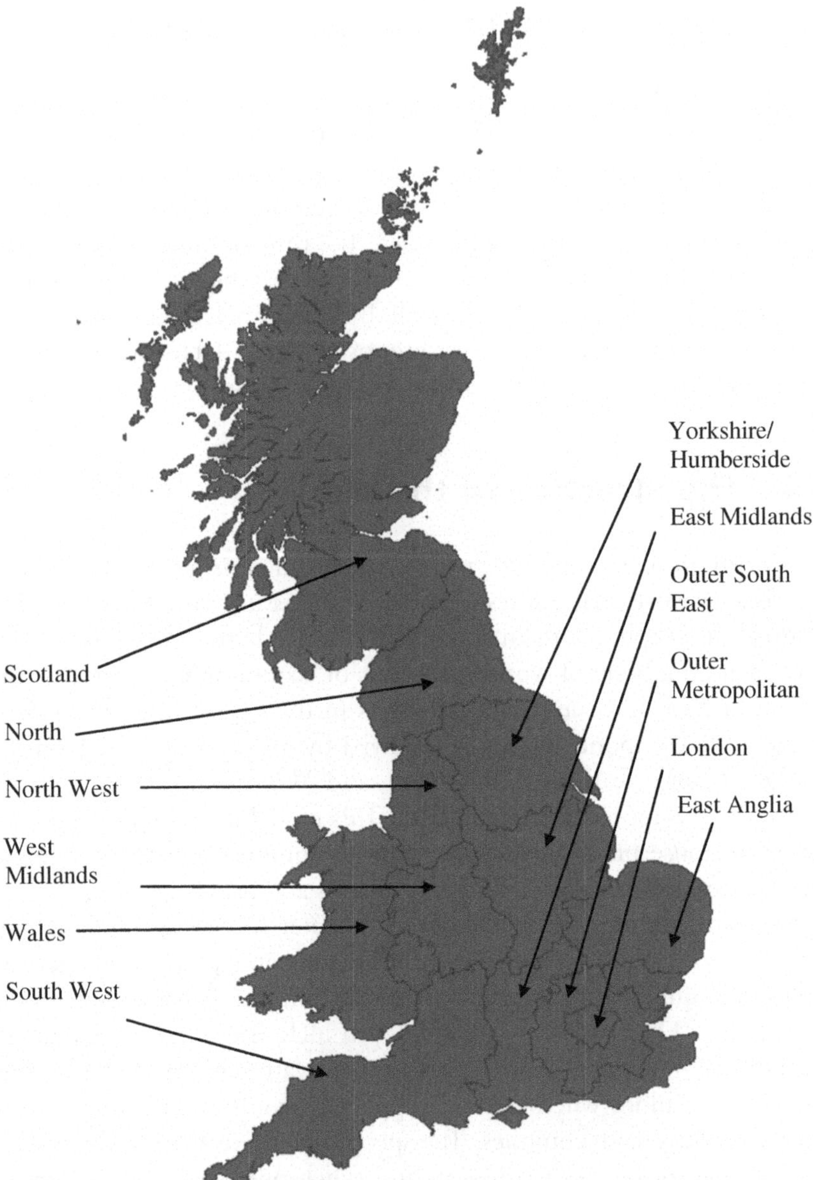

Fig. 1.1 Economic spaces

filter. Its uses and properties are considered in a review of the nature of the data employed.

Another unusual feature of the work is the use of very long series of data. This though limits the range of variables that can be analysed. With a view to consider intensification of the relationship in the second half of the series over the 60 years, house prices and consumption are explored. With the advent of more liberal financing, it is averred by Cutler (1995) that financial deregulation should alter permanently the link between UK household consumption expenditure and housing. The second era, which almost corresponds with the second half of the long period, allows for considerations about the type of consumption and credit. It is the era over which the types of buyer and the ripple effect are considered. It is shown that long-run relations are not in evidence. Cyclical characteristics are in evidence in housing and other associated variables, most commonly in the business cycle range of 5–11 years.

Many of the results echo those found in Goodhart and Hoffman (2008) in revealing RB prices leading FTB and that credit in the 1985–2006 era did not affect output or house price inflation. Drawing from spatial diffusion, a number of explanations of price transmission across buyer groups are proffered. It is concluded that the leadership of housing markets is most likely from expensive to cheaper. London is found to be the leading region and *Modern*, the leading vintage. Drawing from an expectations view, it could be that the more expensive repeat buyer dwelling acts as a marker, signalling changes in cheaper properties. Beyond the leadership issue comes affordability. The top-down explanations for diffusion of price among quality tiers do not recognise the potential dislocation of the FTB as price rises, and yet it appears that FTB and RB numbers are linked. With the bottom-up approach, the repeat buyer's house acquisition is funded, in part, through the affordability of the flat.

It is proposed that two avenues of recycling funds maintain the FTB in the house search. First, the RB feeds the FTB's need for funding through intergenerational transfers. There is possibly a circuit of recycled equity from flat to terraced home to family house and back to flat again. Second, there is evidence that FTBs are crowded out by buy-to-let (BTL) investors. Pryce and Sprigings' (2009) buy-to-let proposition predicts greater volatility within the FTB market and an injection of equity into the flat market. But BTL mortgages are a recent phenomenon. Other than this, one could suggest the great irony of financial liberalisation is that it made housing more affordable temporarily. Before the liberalisation, house hunters found borrowing rationed according to some loyalty metric such as membership of the building society. After the liberalisation, finance is rationed according to income metrics, such as loan to income. Rationing was temporarily suspended.

References

Bogart, W. (1998). *The economics of cities and suburbs*. Upper Saddle River, NJ: Prentice Hall.

Borgersen, T.-A. (2014a). Housing careers house price dispersion and the housing market multiplier. *Housing, Theory and Society, 31*(1), 91–118.

Borgersen, T.-A. (2014b). Equity induced up-trading and the housing market structure. *International Journal of Housing Markets and Analysis, 7*(2), 204–217.

Borgersen, T.-A. (2014c). Heterogeneous housing markets: Structural implications for pricing and risk. *International Journal of Housing Markets and Analysis, 7*(3), 383–396.

Campbell, J., & Mankiw, N. G. (1991). The response of consumption to income: A cross-country investigation. *European Economic Review, 35*(4), 723–756.

Cook, S., & Holly, S. (2000). Statistical properties of UK house prices: An analysis of disaggregated vintages. *Urban Studies, 37*, 2045–2051.

Coulson, N., & McMillen, D. (2007). The dynamics of intraurban quantile house price indexes. *Urban Studies, 44*(8), 1517–1537.

Cutler, J. (1995). The housing market and the economy. *Bank of England Quarterly Bulletin*, August, 260–269.

De Groot, B., & Franses, P. (2008). Stability though cycles. *Technological Forecasting and Social Change, 75*, 301–311.

DiPasquale, D., & Wheaton, W. (1996). *Urban economics and real estate markets*. Englewood Cliffs, NJ: Prentice Hall.

Dusansky, R., & Wilson, R. (1993). The demand for housing: Theoretical considerations. *Journal of Economic Theory, 61*, 120–138.

Gibb, K. (2009). Housing studies and the role of economic theory: An (Applied) disciplinary perspective. *Housing, Theory and Society, 26*(1), 1–26.
Goodhart, C., & Hofmann, B. (2008). House prices, money, credit, and the macroeconomy. *Oxford Review of Economic Policy, 24*(1), 180–205.
Gray, D. (2012). District house price movements in England and Wales 1997–2007: An exploratory spatial data analysis approach. *Urban Studies, 49,* 1411–1434.
Gray, D. (2015). Are prices of new dwellings different? A spectral analysis of UK property vintages. *Cogent Economics and Finance, 3*(1), 1–16.
Ho, L., Ma, Y., & Haurin, D. (2008). House price changes across quality tiers. *Journal of Real Estate Finance & Economics, 37*(4), 299–316.
Hui, H.-C. (2011). Cycles in landed and non-landed housing sub-markets in Malaysia. *International Journal of Housing Markets and Analysis, 4*(2), 144–154.
Mayer, C. (1993). Taxes, income distribution, and the real estate cycle: Why all houses do not appreciate at the same rate. *New England Economic Review,* May/June, 39–50.
Meen, G. (1999). Regional house prices and the ripple effect: A new interpretation. *Housing Studies, 14*(6), 733–753.
Ortalo-Magné, F., & Rady, S. (2006). Housing market dynamics: On the contribution of income shocks and credit constraints. *Review of Economic Studies, 73*(2), 459–485.
Pryce, G., & Evans, G. (2007). *Identifying submarkets at the sub-regional level in England.* London: Department of Communities and Local Government.
Pryce, G., & Sprigings, N. (2009). Outlook for UK housing and the implications for policy: Are we reaping what we have sown? *International Journal of Housing Markets and Analysis, 2*(2), 145–166.
Smith, L., & Ho, M. (1996). The relative price differential between higher and lower priced homes. *Journal of Housing Economics, 5,* 1–17.
Sommervoll, D., Borgersen, T.-A., & Wennemo, T. (2010). Endogenous housing market cycles. *Journal of Banking & Finance, 34*(3), 557–567.
Stein, J. (1995). Prices and trading volume in the housing market: A model with down-payment effects. *The Quarterly Journal of Economics, 110,* 379–405.
Vickerman, R. (1984). *Urban economics.* Salisbury: Philip Allen.

2

A Consideration of Related Contributions in the Fields of Housing and Consumption

Abstract In this chapter, there is a review of literature in various fields of the ripple effect. As a key theme is the role of cycles and co-movement of economic indicators across space, additional literature is drawn from discussions of regional economic integration across Europe. The notion being that methods used at that level could be applied to the regional. Different models of interaction are considered in Chap. 3, in particular, Limtanakool et al.'s overarching framework of nodal interdependence. One can place balanced and imbalanced models within this. As such, monocentric and polycentric urban perspectives can be captured.

Keywords Ripple effect · House prices · Quality of housing · Housing market

2.1 Introduction

In this chapter, there is a review of literature in various fields of the ripple effect. As a key theme is the role of cycles and co-movement of economic indicators across space, additional literature is drawn from

D. Gray, *Cycles in the UK Housing Economy*,
DOI 10.1007/978-3-319-63348-0_2

discussions of regional economic integration across Europe. The notion being that methods used at that level could be applied to the regional. There is also a review of the impact of housing on consumption activity.

2.2 House Price Diffusion Between Buyers, Vintages, and Regions

Three strands of the housing market interaction literature are considered here. There are contributions focused on the buyer, their age, and housing career, such as Ortalo-Magné and Rady (2006), Morrow-Jones and Wenning (2005), and Sommervoll et al. (2010). Second, there are contributions based on the property, such as Coulson and McMillen (2007) and Ho et al. (2008) on differing housing qualities; costliness (Smith and Ho 1996; Smith and Tesarek 1991); and vintage (Cook and Holly 2000; Gray 2015). The third strand features price dispersion across space, often described as the ripple effect (*inter alia*, Alexander and Barrow 1994; Meen 1999; Shi et al. 2009; Wood 2003). The most popular area of research in this strand, the ripple effect in the UK, has it that average regional house price increases are led by London and the South East, spreading to the rest of the country.

2.2.1 UK House Price Ripple Effect

Evidence for the so-called ripple effect in housing comes from Giussani and Hadjimatheou (1991) where it is suggested that house prices in Greater London and the South East increase before those in other regions. Indeed, defining the south as Greater London, South West, South East, and East Anglia, they show the North–South Divide in house prices. They use cross-correlations of annualised quarterly, non-pre-whitened house price changes to reveal lags between movements in Greater London house prices and others. The southern regions of South East and East Anglia are in line, the South West, North West, and East Midlands involve a lag of one period, and the North, Yorkshire/ Humberside, West Midlands, and Scotland have a lag of two. Following on, they use bivariate Granger causality tests to consider causation between the regions and Greater London. South East, South West, and East Anglia exhibited instant causality with Greater London. Otherwise, there is Granger causality from Greater London to all other British regions. As cross-correlations can offer misleading results due to significant serial autocorrelation in either series, pre-whitening is a necessary step, which has not been undertaken.

Hamnett (1988) investigates the relationships between British regional housing markets over the period 1969–1987. Hamnett's description of the pattern of annual UK house price movements suggests that regional growth rates were about the same from 1970 to 1981 and, with the exclusion of Northern Ireland, the house price rankings were stable. It is after this period that the most expensive house price regions, the South East, East Anglia, and the South West, grew more rapidly than the rest. Hamnett goes on to suggest that for the three cycles in his data period, the South East moved into the growth stage and decline stage before the rest, as if the region was out of phase and leading the regional housing system. It appeared then that the south was delinking from the north. It is interesting that house prices in the 1990s in the southern regions had fallen more rapidly than in the north, restoring regional–national house price ratio that Meen (1999) asserts should not exhibit much, if any, of a long-term trend. However, JRF (1995) shows an instability in a North–South East ratio from the 1960s onwards. Thus, the finding of house price convergence, or lack of it, may be period-dependent.

There are numerous cases of papers quoting stable long-run regional relationships. Using UK house price data, Alexander and Barrow (1994) analyse the short-run relationships between pairs of regions using Granger causality tests or, where pairwise cointegration is found, error-correction models. Utilising the 0.1% level of significance, the pairwise Granger causality tests reveal 24 links. Worthington and Higgs (2003) using a different causality method, similar data and period of study, reveal a very small number of regional links in the short run.

Using data from 1969–1995, Munro and Tu (1996) divide the country up into five super-regions: the south, the north, Wales, Northern Ireland, and Scotland. They find that four of the possible ten combinations are cointegrated on a pairwise basis. Notably, Northern Ireland is not cointegrated with any other area; Wales is not cointegrated with other parts of England; and Scotland is cointegrated with the south only. They also undertake a Granger causality anaysis of the housing system, finding that the south Granger causes the north and Wales. No other cases are significant, supporting the notion that the south leads the north. However, given that Scotland (and Northern Ireland) is not involved in either long- or short-run relations, they are separate regions, a point the authors do not explore, but is analysed in Ashworth and Parker (1997).

Holly et al. (2011) apply a spatio-temporal impulse response technique to regional house real price diffusion. They find that London leads the UK with temporal and spatial delays (specifically, a ripple) but also New York prices are found to be weakly exogenous, through London.

The Baumolian approach to convergence, applied initially to countries, starts from a distinction between rich and poor, developed and less developed. The less developed or poor has a low GDP/head, but due to the forces of convergence and the assumption of a common production function, it catches up to the rich level of income at a relatively rapid rate.

Utilising a Baumolian expression, where there are time series and cross-sectional elements, Drake (1995) examines regional house price convergence. Using quarterly data of the logarithm of an UK index of house prices from 1969 to 1993 as the national and the logarithm of South East house prices as the leading region, Drake fails to find a ripple effect from the South East. But he does find evidence of a 'norm differential' between the house prices of the southern and Midlands regions and the South East *outside the Capital.* He highlights the North, East Anglia, and Scotland as the particular regions exhibiting divergent characteristics. Note Drake did not utilise the capital as the leading markets.

A series of articles (Cook 2003, 2005, 2012) considers the dispersion of house prices across the UK. Widespread prevalence of the finding of cointegration is to be expected as the divergence of regional house prices in the 1980s was replaced by convergence in the 1990s. A question for Cook is symmetry across the long-run relationships. Allowing for asymmetry reveals more dimensions in the long-run relationships between house prices in the different regions of the UK. The ripple effect, which implies convergence, is also asymmetric. In Cook (2005), the ripple in the South East occurs first, dispersing gradually to other regions. A decrease in that leading region has a more immediate impact. Cook (2003) finds that Outer South East, East Anglia, and South West experience faster convergence during downswings but other regions, such as the North, North West, West Midlands, and Scotland, exhibit faster rates in upswings. Examining co-movements between London and the other regions, Cook and Watson (2015) reveal a strong correspondence with distance and that London exhibits differing behaviour to other regions during downturns.

Using Pesaran's (2007) pairwise approach to convergence, Abbott and De Vita (2013) find that there is little evidence for convergence among regional house prices. Montagnoli and Nagayasu (2015) find convergence clubs in UK housing of: the South East outer ring plus Northern Ireland; a second is of the Midlands; and the third is of four northern regions. London is distinctive in not converging. This is a trend not a cycle issue but is worth keeping in mind when considering the implications of a ripple effect.

Using the case study of Glasgow again but with repeat sales data, Jones et al. (2003), and then later in the Strathclyde area, and Jones and Leishman (2006) find that, using cointegrated data, sub-markets are stable over time (14 years). They seek to reveal the influence of the leading housing market, Glasgow, in a long-run context within two sub-regional housing market groupings by analysing, in a consideration of cointegration among a group of housing markets areas, whether the addition of the leading region results in an increase in the number of cointegrating vectors. The group ought to be cointegrated, and the addition of the leading region should increase the number of cointegrating relations by [at least] one. They find that the addition of Glasgow adds to the housing system model for the Ayr area but not for the Paisley market.

2.2.2 Contributions Using Other Methods

Using spatial autocorrelation, Gray's (2012) shows a clear ripple effect in the South East/South West/East of England—an area typified as monocentric (De Goei et al. 2010). Holmes (2007), Holmes and Grimes (2008) use region–nation differentials to establish convergence. The latter's focus is principal components analysis and the use of panel unit root tests. They find there is widespread convergence, but Tsai (2014, 2015) does not. Carvalho and Harvey (2005) argue that a unified market exists in this approach when all regions are converging to the national average. If one is diverging, this will affect the reference national average.

McGough and Tsolacos (1995) take the UK commercial property series, detrend them using the Hodrick-Prescott (H-P) filter, and then apply cross-correlations to expose delays. Jin and Grissom (2008) apply the H-P filter to separate trend from the cyclical component in house prices. Using an ARMA model combined with the extracted trend, they forecast house prices in US cities.

2.2.3 Revealing House Price Diffusion in Other Countries

Stevenson (2004) utilises second-hand house prices for the Irish urban areas of Dublin, Cork, Galway, Limerick, Waterford plus the residual, rural. He provides a detailed description of the Irish housing market. His method entails city pairwise and multi-variate error correction models (ECM). He finds three out of a potential five common trends, suggesting the Irish city housing market areas are reasonably closely bonded together in the long run (Dickey et al. 1991).

When considering Granger causality tests on a multi-variate basis, Stevenson finds that Dublin is not a clear leader of all others. Rather, it causes a change in the 'Rural' that Granger-causes change in the others. Citing Alexander and Barrow (1994), Stevenson believes that the rural market acts as an extension of Dublin's 'reach'. Dublin is the only time series that Granger-causes all others on a bivariate basis and is not Granger-caused itself, and so appears as the leading region.

Berg (2002) finds that there is a leading city in the Swedish system; that of Stockholm, over a range of periodicities from a month to a year. However, with the exception of 'Sparsely Populated', Stockholm is found to be Granger-caused by each one of the other residential variables used, leaving the lingering question about Granger causality and leadership: Which leads which market?

Luo et al. (2007) find that, using a pairwise error correction approach, there is a hierarchy in the diffusion pattern of house prices among Australian state capital cities, with Sydney at the top level, followed by Melbourne, then Perth and Adelaide, and finally, another four cities. Diffusion is not necessarily related to size/urban hierarchy or an inverse function of distance. For example, Brisbane is the third city by population and is relatively close to Sydney but is placed at the bottom of their city hierarchy. They find more causal links between non-contiguous regions than contiguous ones, and that prices are, in part, driven by local economic growth. Luo et al. conclude that it is not the largest market that drives all others; no housing market is subject to a distinctive trend; and the markets are bonded in the long run, to what extent is not clear. Wilson and Zurbruegg (2008), Tu (2000) find a segmented Australian housing market space, where prices are driven by internal factors, such as earnings. On a pairwise basis, Tu (2000) finds few cases of Granger causality among Australian capitals but there is a 'ripple' from Brisbane, through Sydney to Melbourne.

Authors using US house price data find house price diffusion among neighbouring but not non-neighbouring tracts (Pollakowski and Ray 1997; Dolde and Tirtiroglu 1997). This is suggestive of the information from other territories feeding into local prices. However, there is no national ripple effect. Perhaps that is a function of the size of the USA and the large tracts of empty space between urban areas.

Lee and Chien (2011) find that Taiwan's regional house prices exhibit a long-run relationship except with Taipei City. The authors use three cities and Taipei City's hinterland, Taipei County, whose average house prices are above the other cities in the study. There is long-run but not short-run causality from the other cities to Taipei City, which is a result inconsistent with an integrated national housing market system. Taipei County feeds back with Taipei City and Granger-causes Taichung City, a local housing market area. Interestingly, when applying different techniques to the same data, Chen et al. (2011) find that Taipei City is found not to be cointegrated with the rest of the housing market system, suggesting a segmented market again.

Using Finnish data, Oikarinen (2006) finds that housing price changes diffuse first from the country's main economic centre, the Helsinki Metropolitan Area, to regional centres, and then to the peripheral areas. This is consistent with an urban system thesis. His explanation for this, though, relates to information asymmetries between professional market agents concentrated in the metropolitan areas and others in the periphery.

2.2.4 Price Interaction Between Housing Markets of Different Quality

Coulson and McMillen (2007) posit that there is a house price ripple effect related to the quality of housing. The most expensive house prices, assessed by quantile, lead the next quantile down, and that leads the one below it, and so on in a Granger causality sense. They also test for cointegration with a view to expose a long-run equilibrium between five different qualities of housing. Positing that there are only one or two common shocks driving house prices, they anticipate that the number of cointegrating vectors will be three or four. Using house price indices for three municipalities near Chicago, USA, they find that the prices of lower quality houses are Granger-caused by higher quality ones but not the reverse. They also find that the five indices for each of the three areas are cointegrated.

Hui (2011) explores segments of housing markets in Malaysia. Using a Baxter-King and a Christiano and Fitzgerald filter, he decomposes deflated dwelling price indices into trend and cyclical components. He establishes temporal delays between sub-markets of condominiums, terraced, semi-detached, and detached residential accommodation. Cross-correlations of the cyclical components indicate that non-landed dwelling prices lead landed ones. In-sample Granger causality tests and Theil's U for out-of-sample forecasting suggest the modelling of the landed dwelling prices is improved when condominiums' values are included in terraced and semi-detached models. He argues that this form of real estate is more likely to be seen as an investment than the others. With a lead of one to two quarters, investors can make profit from terraced and semi-detached properties.

At odds with Hui and Coulson and McMillen, Ho et al. (2008) find the reverse. Granger causality tests indicate that lower quality housing in Hong Kong drives higher quality ones. There is no feedback.

DiPasquale and Wheaton do not imply a direction of price change between quality tiers, only an equilibrating system that drives long-run prices to have a stable differential. Levin and Pryce (2009) find that inequalities between high- and low-cost housing market areas are cyclical.

There are a number of contributions to the quality hierarchy related to types of buyers. Borgersen (2014a, b) adds to the OMR framework a mix in between the flat and the house an intermediate [terraced] dwelling: thus, there are two trade-up homes, rather than one. Price amplification emerges through its dispersion between the steps of the housing ladder. A positive [income] shock to a flat affects the other two correspondingly. However, because an owner vacates a property when they move up, a shock to intermediate homes has a positive effect on houses but a negative impact on flats. A shock to houses affects the other two negatively. In other words, there is an asymmetry in the shock response. It has a positive effect upward, and a negative one downward. As the equity in the top segment has no outlet, which is consistent with Eichholtz and Lindenthal (2014), the house does not have an amplifier effect.

OMR presumes that a FTB purchase takes place when the flat can be afforded. There is no stock of vacant houses, so this purchase affects the house market. OMR proposes that a rise in income affecting the flat market may lead to an overreaction in the house market. Steady state flat prices are proportional to the endowments (income) of FTBs, whereas steady state house prices rise less than proportionally with endowments but more in absolute terms than flat prices. The differential expands. Benito (2006) notes that price instability in the OMR model can arise through volatility in income, particularly the marginal FTBs. Their participation will also be sensitive to changes in credit rationing.

The financial accelerator would favour those with assets (Aoki et al. 2004), which implies that RB dwellings would accelerate more rapidly than FTBs' (Borgersen 2014a, b; Meen 2011; OMR; Smith and Ho 1996; Smith and Tesarek 1991; Stein 1995), expanding the differentials between the tiers as price rises.

With Sommervoll et al. (2010), it is lack of buyer-interest that leads to selling price being revised, which could be foreseen by the vendor, suggesting this price signalling proposition is not inconsistent with their model. Indeed, as cycles in Sommervoll et al. are a function of adaptive price expectations, how price expectations are updated is crucial for cycle periodicities. If expectations are slow to adjust and feature local information overspill, then the cycles of one market could affect another's, possibly with a delay.

Pryce and Sprigings (2009) make the point that, as far as the life cycle/housing career is concerned, a father or mother buying a dwelling at the age of 25, having a child at 30, dying at 80, leaves that child with the possibility of inheriting the parental dwelling at 55, just about the same time that their mortgage is paid off. Fifty-five would be a life cycle's peak earnings period, so an intergeneration transfer of wealth to a FTB is far from improbable.

Borgersen (2014c) focuses on price volatility (risk) and intergenerational equity transfers. Here, a shock to house market affects flat prices through bequests, gifts, or housing equity release transfers, accelerating their rate of appreciation to be above that of houses. If intergenerational transfers and a trading down to a bungalow are included in the mix, there are outlets for the equity from the top segment in Borgersen (2014a). Indeed, trading down in price does not necessarily mean a smaller dwelling. Consistent with the second ripple strand, geographical migration could release equity whilst preserving the ownership of a four-bedroomed family home, spreading wealth to lower priced regions. Importantly, there is a feedback loop: a positive shock to flats, terraced, and houses will be amplified and affects all other parts of the property market. With the assistance of parents, the FTB can continue to join the housing ladder when normally out-priced, so that equity growth can be self-refreshing. This feedback can be possible within OMR's model. It is conceivable that a housing hierarchy/ladder can be maintained without many FTBs. When trading down, a housing series or chain could entail a RB selling a house and purchasing a flat, which funds someone else's terraced house procurement, which facilitates the acquisition of the house by a third party.

Using US data, Luea (2008) finds that gifts enhance households' property demand by 9–11% so that the acquisition entails a more expensive property with a greater housing cost burden. Mayer and Engelhardt (1996) and Engelhardt and Mayer (1994) find that a quarter of FTBs receive some familial financial support, supplying, on average, half of the deposit. Clarke (2011a) suggests that intergenerational transfers make up a significant but stable volume of mortgages. There were an estimated 31,000 UK FTBs that were 'assisted' in the second quarters of both 2005 and 2011, and yet the number of unassisted FTBs dropped by 78% to 16,000 over the same six years. So, whilst the number of 'assisted' FTBs remained stable, the 'assisted' proportion rose from 31 to 66%. More recently, Clarke (2015) estimated the proportion of unassisted FTBs stood at 38% in 2014, which is around the rate post-2008 in Clarke (2011a). The added complication was two Help-to-Buy programmes providing additional support. Notably, consistent with Luea (2008), the assisted FTB in 2014 bought a more expensive abode (£175,000) with a smaller loan (£120,000) than the unassisted (£147,000; £129,000).

An additional innovation during financial liberalisation in the fourth phase of Meen (2011) is the buy-to-let (BTL) mortgage. Pryce and Sprigings (2009) find that, as BTL purchasers occupy the same portion of the housing market as FTBs, purchasing a dwelling for rent sucks flats out of the owner-occupation market, possibly being rented to those that would have bought. The BTL mortgage began life in 1995 but since 1999, 90% have been taken out during periods of above-trend price increases (Pryce and Sprigings 2009). Clarke (2011b) disputes the claim about FTB displacement, making the point that these purchases are highly localised, in cities, possibly serving a student market. Also, the greater renting sector caters for the notable recent rise in the population of migrants in the UK.

Gregoriou et al. (2014) find that lending is decoupling from earnings and the duration of a repayment mortgage is drifting from 25 to 35 years (Giles 2016), with a quarter of first-time buyers taking out a 35-year mortgage in 2015 facilitating this. The Bank of England has imposed some limits on lending ratios but not on repayment periods.

It is worried by the implications of repayment period extending into retirement. This oversight allows for FTBs to afford the unobtainable dwelling, consistent with a Leamer-Minky-type criticism of financial regulation facilitating boosted house prices.

Cook and Holly (2000) consider whether there are common trends and cycles among *Older, Modern*, and *New* UK house prices. *New* housing is not cointegrated with second-hand housing on a pairwise basis. Non-synchronised, common cycles are found among the three series. This is interpreted as differential reactions to a common shock. They do not consider a ripple effect in these cycles. They find that *New* housing is more volatile, showing a tendency to rise more rapidly and to higher peaks relative to troughs. They explain this as the ability of owners of second-hand dwellings to hold on to their properties in a downturn. This runs counter to one of the premises in the work presented here: *New* should be less volatile than second-hand because of this. Using Spectral Analysis over 60 years, Gray (2015) finds a minor five and a major 7½-year cycle. He proposes that the pricing could be seen as supply-led (five-year cycle) or demand-driven (7½-year cycle). Or that the five year is more strongly linked to the FTB and the RB second-hand cycle lasts 7½ years. Contrary to Cook and Holly, *New* is found to have lower volatility, and *New* leads *Modern* which precedes *Older* dwellings.

2.3 How Long Are Economic Cycles?

De Groot and Franses (2012) and Jadevicius and Huston (2014) review papers that estimate cycles in socio-economic indicators. The latter pair catalogue major and auxiliary business cycles, whereas the former pair focus on contributions in the longer cycle range.

De Groot and Franses (2008) argue that long-term economic stability comes from the persistence of multiple, robust cycles that enables the 'system' to absorb exogenous shocks that would otherwise put mature economies 'off balance'. Revealing cycles of 10.3, 25.7, 57.7, and 92 years across four economies, the 10.3-year cycle is the most common with a probability that an economic variable would have such a cycle of over 0.5. They illustrate how an economic series could be described by [a pair of] independent cycles. If they were harmonics of each other, there would be a notable long cycle reflecting the lowest frequency. Higher harmonics would be subject to interference, so be obscured. Where the [two] cycles are not harmonics, this interference would be much reduced. Overall, they conclude that an economic cycle could be represented by a few frequencies. Sanidas (2014) reveals four harmonic series in the fluctuations of the Australian Dollar. It, along with the New Zealand and Canadian Dollars, and the Norwegian Krone, is deemed a commodity currency, which is strongly affected by world price of their key export(s).

Agénor et al. (2000) find output fluctuations across developed and industrial countries have many similarities. Marchand (1981) reveals local cycles, which he defines as a set of impulses originating from industrial requirements of certain urban economies, whose rapid but limited impact is transmitted through import–export ties.

Calderon and Fuentes (2014) find that business cycles have changed over the 22 years to 2007. Studying 71 countries from 1970 of which 23 are developed, they find that recessions are steeper and costlier in developing economies and in the globalised/financial liberalised era (the great moderation 1985–2007), they are less so for both groups. Also, financial cycles precede real cycles. They use the Harding-Pagan approach to turning points in time series. Investment and consumption resemble real GDP dynamics but the former more, and the latter less, volatile. Across the 23, GDP has a cycle of around 28 and the UK around 30 quarters or 7½ years.

Wunder (2012) suggests a change in business cycle drivers. Rather than investment which has been the norm since 1950, he avers that the last two cycles were driven by consumer activity. This consumer activity is funded by debt held by the top 20% of the income distribution. Thus, in the liberal era, consumption drives income.

Financial cycles are also of importance, not least as these are heavily associated with crises. Schularick and Taylor (2012) and Aikman et al. (2014) examine longer series using loans as a measure of credit. This is outstanding lending to corporates and households, both secured and unsecured. The former conclude credit aggregates contain valuable information about the likelihood of future financial crises. The economist's view that money is merely a veil should be called into question. Aikman et al. find a 13⅓-year periodicity in credit within a 130-year series of UK data. This periodicity in credit is consistent with the eras of Meen (2011) and Scanlon and Whitehead (2011). In the longer run, the longer cycles in house prices and credit, which appear as trends when analysed over a few decades, could have 'common trends'.

Aikman et al. suggest that UK real loans or credit provision is pro-cyclical, with an amplitude twice that of the general business cycle, as proxied by real GDP, but a periodicity, which is twice as long as the one for GDP. Moreover, they find a minor cycle of 4½ years in duration. Variations in GDP do not account much for perturbations in credit (Aikman et al. 2014). Goodhart and Hoffman (2008) find that neither broad money nor credit in the 1985–2006 era affects output or house price inflation. Income and house prices are mutually reinforcing; the former does not Granger-cause money supply, but the latter do.

Drehmann et al. (2012) consider the cyclical characteristics of credit, credit/GDP, house prices, equity prices, and GDP, across seven OECD countries including the UK. They find that cycles of between 8 and 30 years are more important than those of shorter periodicities in characterising the variables' behaviour. In keeping with other authors, the cycles are possibly twice as long post-1985 compared with before. Creating a composite of property prices and credit, a financial cycle of sixteen years is found to correspond well with financial crises, not far from the 13 of Aikman et al..

Iacoviello and Pavan (2013) compare the US housing market during the great moderation and the great recession. They find that when credit constraints are relaxed, aggregate volatility is reduced but idiosyncratic volatility rises. Lower down payments should smooth housing demand but higher risk should deter buyers from purchasing larger dwellings. Using a H-P filter, they reveal that real GDP, consumption, housing investment (construction) and debt all exhibit a fall in the degree of cyclicality in the period 1983–2010 compared with 1952–1982. The divide reflects differing eras of financial constraints and borrowing. Consistent with the permanent income hypothesis, consumption is far less volatile than income. Housing investment (construction) has 2.5× the volatility of income in both eras. Debt does not alter much.

They find that household mortgage debt is highly pro-cyclical in the 30 years from 1952 with a correlation of 0.78. This drops to 0.43 in the 28 years after 1982, suggesting that an income criteria or constraint is loosened. If, as they claim, this is driven in part by impatient, constrained buyers moving when times are good, this puts housing in the same category as durable goods in general. Housing investment is also highly pro-cyclical with a correlation of 0.89 in the first period, dropping to 0.75 in the second.

2.3.1 Evidence of Cycles in Property

Property is an asset class where periods of under and over supply are the norm (DiPasquale and Wheaton 1996; Pyhrr et al. 1999). Using univariate spectral analysis, common cycles among stock indices of the property sector in Singapore, Hong Kong, Malaysia, Japan, and the UK of about 2½–4 years are exposed by Liow (2007). Chen et al. (2004) reveal two or three hidden periodicities in house price series from Hong Kong, Singapore, Taipei, and Tokyo from 1976 to 1998. They find a business cycle (of around 7.9–10.4 years), an intermediate cycle (3.2–4.4 years), and an annual cycle. They describe the business cycle as driven by exogenous shocks and the four-year periodicity as an endogenous production lag cycle. Alexander and Barrow (1994) and Rosenthal (1986) find a five to ten and six to eight year periodicity, respectively, in UK regional house prices. Wilson and Okunev (1999) reveal high cospectra values between real estate investment trusts and financial assets markets at cycles of 3 years in Australia, 3½ in the USA, and 6 and 8 years in UK series.

The Royal Institute of Chartered Surveyors finds cycles in UK property of around 8 years, with possibly two periodicities of five and nine years (Royal Institute of Chartered Surveyors (RICS) 1999). Indeed, Reed and Wu (2010) state that property cycles are 'unavoidable'. Pugh and Dehesh (2001) point out that property cycles can be separated into endogenous and exogenous: the former because of long lead times in construction; the latter concerns the strong link between property and the wider macro-economy. Pritchett (1984) posits that, despite a common national house price cycle, there are separate, non-coincident ones of distinct types of property. The supply of property lags demand, with cycle turning points occurring when the growth of the two are in opposite directions.

DiPasquale and Wheaton (1996) present a model of house prices incorporating simple price expectations that predicts cyclical behaviour without periodic exogenous variables driving them. Leamer (2007, 2015) argues that business cycles are housing cycles.

Filtering is common. Stevenson et al. (2014) and Akimov et al. (2015) employ a mean corrected index of concordance to assess the degree of commonality in property cycles. In the 2015 paper, they also decompose series into unobserved trend and cycle using a Hodrick-Prescott and a Beverage-Nelson filter, correlating the detrended series. Agnello and Schuknecht (2011) use a 10,000 H-P smoothing parameter to reveal an upward and a downward UK house price trend of seven years each, consistent with Bracke conclusions about long cycles. Cyclical deviations from trend are used to 'define' housing bubble events. Bracke identifies 1989Q2 and 2007Q4 as peaks and 1996Q2 as a trough in UK house prices. Agnello and Schuknecht (2011) suggest the growth phase of 1983–1989 and 1997–2004, with a decline phase of 1990–1996. There are two sets of turning points: long and short term. The long-term undulations can be identified as 1983–1989, 1989–1996, 1996–2005, and 2005+.

Using spectral analysis, Barras and Ferguson (1985) find a major and a minor cycle for almost all the UK property construction series they examine. For example, there is a 6½-year major cycle and a 15-quarter minor cycle in private housing construction and a nine-year periodicity in private commercial property construction commissioning.

Rosenthal (1986) uses cross-spectral analysis to examine UK regional house price cycles in the period 1975–1981. He finds that at lower frequencies coherence was high with insignificant phase between regions and the nation. He also concludes that there is not much evidence that neighbouring regions are more closely related than non-neighbours.

Leamer (2007) argues that there is a US house sale volume rather than a price cycle that matters. This applies to both existing and new housing. Leamer (2015) shows existing house prices peaked in April 2007, 19 months after volume had begun to decline. Volume also picked up in January 2008, 15 months before prices. However, volume has not the long-run trend seen in prices.

Although adaptive expectations modelling can be viewed as not in keeping with homo economicus, DiPasquale and Wheaton (1996) cite evidence for this form of price forecasting by economic agents, and it does generate house price cycles, overshooting and bursting bubbles. In a review of three major asset price bubbles, Spotton (1997) draws a number of conclusion, amongst which include the formation of expectations of future capital gains was based on past price increases, not future income streams. Bubbles were fuelled by the availability of credit, probably borrowed against the assets whose prices were subject to speculation. Clayton (1998) also finds evidence supporting this notion of naïve forecasts in US real-estate markets. McDonald (1985) concludes that the expectation of nominal price increase has a significant impact on the current price. Importantly, this expectation is based on the past growth rates of prices in neighbouring areas—overspill.

DiPasquale and Wheaton propose that house prices will be affected by new household formation. Meen (1998) considers the role of demographic change on the UK housing market and how it is modelled. He concludes demography would have no effect on either owner–occupation or prices. It is possible that increased demand (or need) is accommodated by the private rental sector or in social housing. However, he raises concerns about house supply. He finds that price elasticity of housing supply in the UK is low. Unless the nature of the construction industry and the land-use planning system changes substantially, improvements in the economy performance will lead to higher house prices rather than to higher owner–occupier rates. In both Bover et al. (1989) and DiPasquale and Wheaton, it is housing supply that bursts the bubble. If new supply is slow to respond, house prices could rise propitiously before the bubble bursts, suggesting a long 'carrier wave' cycle.

2.3.2 International Cycles

Fatas (1997) suggests regional specialisation leads to: asymmetric, industry-specific, shocks; distinct regional cycles; and differences in sensitivity to economic policy initiatives. Marchand (1981) suggests that employment variations at the (Canadian) urban level are affected by a pervasive business cycle. Local demand conditions that reflect the industrial structure are transmitted through intercity trading ties as minor cycles. This implies that trade is not a driver of common business cycles. At a higher, less integrated level, Camacho et al. (2008) find transmission national cycle through trade, but De Haan et al. (2008) question the integration mechanism of trade. Trade intensity only explains a fraction of business cycle correlation.

By examining business cycles across Eurozone members, Artis and Zhang (1997) test for OCA tendencies. They examine synchronicity and linkage cross-correlations between the German hegemon and ERM members. This core-periphery view among European countries is the prevailing one, yet Camacho et al. (2008) do not find evidence to support this perspective. De Haan et al. (2008) conclude that business cycle synchronisation in Europe increased post-1990, but there is no strong evidence of European business cycles *becoming* more synchronised. Despite membership of a single currency, the emergence of a European cycle is not found.

Wynne and Koo (2000) consider measures of business cycles across 15 EU countries and the USA. They review the correlations of the cyclical component using a Baxter and King filter, capturing up to 8-year cycles in aggregate output. There are many cases of no correlation. The UK cycle is linked to the big economies. Notably, it is not linked to Ireland's. As there is a large open border, this is unexpected. They consider employment cycles. Here, Ireland *is* linked to the UK. They find that inflation is not well synchronised in Europe. However, the UK's prices reflect output in being linked to the big economies. The UK is more strongly linked to the USA than to Europe on these measures.

2.4 Consumption over a Life Time

In their identification of influences on consumption, horizons are considered by Attanasio and Browning (1995). They identify lifetime income effects, cohort effects, life-cycle effects, cyclical effects, and heterogeneity effects. Lifetime income refers to the profile of earnings over the lifetime. Fernández-Villaverde and Krueger (2002) reveal the lifetime profile of income expenditure for overlapping generations, which turns out to be an inverted-*U* shape. An employment career captures the notion of a progression, where seniority, responsibilities, and salary rise with time. Income rises with age from a low in the 20s. In mid-life, earnings rise to a peak around the age of 55. They then tend to decline, reflecting how some prepare early for retirement.

Eichholtz and Lindenthal (2014) also reveal the inverted-*U* shape in income in English household earnings, with a peak at 52 years. Although income may be different across groups subdivided by qualifications, the inverted-*U* is a common profile. The consumption of housing is tied to this profile. They show that lot size is not important; it is interior space that varies with age, and by implication, income.

Peersman and Pozzi (2007) recommend greater attention to short-term fluctuations in consumption research. Recessions, they find, are characterised by higher consumption sensitivity to income. Coinciding with the liberalisation era, unemployment hysteresis in Europe should discourage consumers' consumption and boost precautionary savings. Sun et al. (2007) show that house prices affect consumption significantly in Singapore. The link found is around 25 quarters, in the business cycle range, rather than longer periodicities where permanent or life-cycle factors would be captured. Contrasting with Peersman and Pozzi, the capital gain effect is stronger during a boom than a recession period.

2.4.1 The Consumption and Housing Nexus

Using UK data, Bagliano and Morana (2010) subdivided house price fluctuations into transitory and permanent. They do not find cointegration among house prices and consumption, also implying no long-term relationship. Using Swedish data and guided by a life-cycle model, Yang and Wang (2012) find that house prices are temporarily affected by transitory shocks (two years) and consumption is more or less immune. It takes two years for house prices to absorb an interest rate shock, whereas consumption responds negatively. Lettau and Ludvigson (2004) find that contrary to conventional wisdom, the vast majority of quarterly fluctuations in asset values are attributable to transitory innovations that display virtually no association with consumption, contemporaneously, or at any future date. By contrast, aggregate consumption expenditure is affected by permanent changes in wealth. This is consistent with the PIH as the asset value changes are not perceived as permanent.

Li and Yao (2007) find that the young and the old are more house price sensitive than the middle-aged. All increase their consumption following a rise in price but not all benefit. The young see a longer future housing consumption and higher housing costs. Older owners have a short horizon; they seek to capture capital gains to boost non-housing consumption. It is they that experience a welfare benefit from a price rise; the young, lose, with 'breakeven' occurring around the age of 60.

Renters' consumption is affected by house price. Sheiner (1995) finds that young people who rent increase their savings between $27 and 76 for every $100 rise in average house price. She concludes that the house purchase down payment is a prime motivator for saving.

Benito and Wood (2005) discuss the impact of house moving on consumption. Using survey data from the British Household Panel Survey, motivated partly to 'match' the characteristics of their newly purchased property, they find two to three times increase in the likelihood of purchasing certain durable goods when moving home compared with a 'stayer'.

2.4.2 Credit Constraints: Constrained Consumption

Bacchetta and Gerlach (1997) consider the impact of credit liberalisation on a range of countries. UK consumption growth is found to be more strongly associated with credit growth than income growth. One possible explanation is that, by relaxing borrowing constraints, the credit liberalisation process increased substantially the desired level of current consumption. In the adjustment period, consumption grows faster than usual.

Campbell and Mankiw (1991) present a simple model to explain consumption that combines permanent and current incomes. A relaxation of a financial constraint allows consumers to behave, as the permanent income hypothesis suggests, smooth over a long horizon. Analysing a collection of developed countries, they find that, apart from in the UK, liquidity constraints did not decline in importance. Chen et al. (2010) also discuss the implications of two groups within a PIH-LC framework. One group is constrained financially and the other is not. The former is limited to consuming what is currently affordable (cash-on-hand), whereas the other can borrow to smooth consumption across a longer period. Using a threshold model, shifting from one to the other should boost current consumption. A boost to income would increase consumption directly and shift some from less to more creditworthy. A rising dwelling value as a source of additional collateral could be another means of switching. This position has profound implications. The PIH-LC framework posits that consumption should be smoothed relative to income.

To add richness to this analysis, Chen et al. (2010) consider durable and non-durable consumption and unsecured lending. Unsecured lending is found to be unresponsive to house prices. They find that durables are affected by house prices for those that are credit-constrained. Also, durables are affected by changes in incomes. Indeed, Campbell and Cocco (2007) find a significant relationship between real house prices and non-durable consumption growth.

References

Abbott, A., & De Vita, G. (2013). Testing for long-run convergence across regional house prices in the UK: A pairwise approach. *Applied Economics, 45,* 1227–1238.

Agénor, P.-R., Prasad, E., & McDermott, C. (2000). Macroeconomic fluctuations in developing countries—Some stylized facts. *World Bank Economic Review, 14*(2), 251–285.

Agnello, L., & Schuknecht, L. (2011). Booms and busts in housing markets: Determinants and implications. *Journal of Housing Economics, 20*(4), 171–190.

Aikman, D., Haldane, A., & Nelson, B. (2014, June). Curbing the credit cycle. *The Economic Journal, 125,* 1072–1109.

Akimov, A., Stevenson, S., & Young, J. (2015). Synchronisation and commonalities in metropolitan housing market cycles. *Urban Studies, 52*(9), 1665–1682.

Alexander, C., & Barrow, M. (1994). Seasonality and cointegration of regional house prices in the UK. *Urban Studies, 31,* 1667–1689.

Aoki, K., Proudmand, J., & Vlieghe, G. (2004). House prices, consumption and monetary policy: A financial accelerator approach. *Journal of Financial Intermediation, 13,* 414–435.

Artis, M., & Zhang, W. (1997). International business cycles and the ERM: Is there a European business cycle? *International Journal of Finance and Economics, 2,* 1–16.

Ashworth, J., & Parker, S. (1997). Modelling regional house prices in the UK. *Scottish Journal of Political Economy, 44,* 225–246.

Attanasio, O., & Browning, M. (1995). Consumption over the Life Cycle and over the Business Cycle. *American Economic Review, 85,* 1118–1137.

Bacchetta, P., & Gerlach S. (1997). Consumption and credit constraints: International evidence. *Journal of Monetary Economics, 40,* 207–238.

Bagliano, F., & Morana, C. (2010). Business cycle comovement in the G-7: Common shocks or common transmission mechanisms? *Applied Economics, 42*(18), 2327–2345.

Barras, R., & Ferguson, D. (1985). A spectral analysis of building cycles in Britain. *Environment and Planning A, 17,* 1369–1391.

Benito, A. (2006, March). *How does the down-payment constraint affect the UK housing market* (Bank of England Working Paper 294).

Benito, A., & Wood, R. (2005). How important is housing market activity for durables spending? *Bank of England Quarterly Bulletin, 45*(2), 153–159.

Berg, L. (2002). Prices on the second hand market for Swedish family houses. *European Journal of Housing Policy, 2*(1), 1–24.

Borgersen, T.-A. (2014a). Housing careers, house price dispersion and the housing market multiplier. *Housing, Theory and Society, 31*(1), 91–118.

Borgersen, T.-A. (2014b). Equity induced up-trading and the housing market structure. *International Journal of Housing Markets and Analysis, 7*(2), 204–217.

Borgersen, T.-A. (2014c). Heterogeneous housing markets: Structural implications for pricing and risk. *International Journal of Housing Markets and Analysis, 7*(3), 383–396.

Bover, O., Muellbauer, J., & Murphy, A. (1989). Housing, wages and UK labour markets. *Oxford Bulletin of Economics and Statistics, 51,* 367–382.

Calderon, C., & Fuentes, J. (2014). Have business cycle changed over the last two decades? An empirical investigation. *Journal of Development Studies, 109,* 98–123.

Camacho, M., Perez-Quiros, G., & Saiz, L. (2008). Do European business cycles look like one? *Journal of Economic Dynamics and Control, 32*(7), 2165–2190.

Campbell, J., & Cocco, J. (2007). How do house prices affect consumption? Evidence from micro data. *Journal of Monetary Economics, 54*(3), 591–621.

Campbell, J., & Mankiw, N. G. (1991). The response of consumption to income: A cross-country investigation. *European Economic Review, 35*(4), 723–756.

Carvalho, V., & Harvey, A. (2005). Growth, cycles and convergence in US regional time series. *International Journal of Forecasting, 21*, 667–686.

Chen, M.-C., Kawaguchi, Y., & Patel, K. (2004). An analysis of the trends and cyclical behaviours of house prices in the Asian markets. *Journal of Property Investment & Finance, 22*(1), 55–75.

Chen, N.-K., Chen, S.-S., & Chou, Y.-H. (2010). House prices, collateral constraints, and the asymmetric effect on consumption. *Journal of Housing Economics, 19*, 26–37.

Chen, P.-F., Chien, M.-S., & Lee, C.-C. (2011). Dynamic modeling of regional house price diffusion in Taiwan. *Journal of Housing Economics, 20*(4), 315–332.

Clarke, B. (2011a, December 14). *First-time buyers and affordability: A fresh perspective* [press release]. Council of Mortgage Lenders. http://www.cml.org.uk/news/390/. Accessed 29 June 2015.

Clarke, B. (2011b, November 16). *What's driving buy-to-let* [press release]. Council of Mortgage Lenders. http://www.cml.org.uk/news/382/. Accessed 29 June 2015.

Clarke, B. (2015, March 5). *New CML data shows nearly half of first-time buyers didn't use the 'bank of mum and dad'* [press release]. Council of Mortgage Lenders. http://www.cml.org.uk/news/712/. Accessed 29 June 2015.

Clayton, J. (1998). Further evidence on real estate market efficiency. *The Journal of Real Estate Research, 15*(1/2), 41–57.

Cook, S. (2003). The convergence of regional house prices in the UK. *Urban Studies, 40*(11), 2285–2294.

Cook, S. (2005). Detecting long-run relationships in regional house prices in the UK. *International Review of Applied Economics, 19*(1), 107–118.

Cook, S. (2012). β-convergence and the cyclical dynamics of UK regional house prices. *Urban Studies, 49*(1), 203–218.

Cook, S., & Holly, S. (2000). Statistical properties of UK house prices: An analysis of disaggregated vintages. *Urban Studies, 37*, 2045–2051.

Cook, S., & Watson, D. (2015). A new perspective on the ripple effect in the UK housing market: Co-movement, cyclical subsamples and alternative indices. *Urban Studies, 53*(14), 3048–3062.

Coulson, N., & McMillen, D. (2007). The dynamics of intraurban quantile house price indexes. *Urban Studies, 44*(8), 1517–1537.

De Goei, B., Burger, M., Van Oort, F., & Kitson, M. (2010). Functional polycentrism and urban network development in the greater South East, United Kingdom: Evidence from commuting patterns, 1981–2001. *Regional Studies, 44*(9), 1149–1170.

De Groot, B., & Franses, P. (2008). Stability though cycles. *Technological Forecasting and Social Change, 75,* 301–311.

De Groot, B., & Franses, P. (2012). Common socio-economic cycle periods. *Technological Forecasting and Social Change, 79*(1), 59–68.

De Haan, J., Inklaar, R., & Jong-A-Pin, R. (2008). Will business cycles in the Euro area converge? A critical survey of empirical research. *Journal of Economic Surveys, 22*(2), 234–273.

Dickey, D., Jansen, D., & Thornton, D. (1991). A primer on cointegration with an application to money and income. *Federal Reserve Bank of St. Louis,* March/April, 58–78.

DiPasquale, D., & Wheaton, W. (1996). *Urban economics and real estate markets*. Englewood Cliffs, NJ: Prentice Hall.

Dolde, W., & Tirtiroglu, D. (1997). Temporal and spatial information diffusion in real estate price changes and variances. *Real Estate Economics, 25*(4), 539–565.

Drake, L. (1995). Testing for convergence between UK regional house prices. *Applied Economics, 29,* 357–366.

Drehmann, M., Borio, C., & Tstasaronis, K. (2012, June). *Characterising the financial cycle: Don't lose sight of the medium term!* (BIS Working Papers No. 380). Bank for International Settlements.

Eichholtz, P., & Lindenthal, T. (2014). Demographics, human capital and the demand for housing. *Journal of Housing Economics, 26*(2), 19–32.

Engelhardt, G., & Mayer, C. (1994). Gifts for home purchase and housing market behavior. *New England Economic Review,* May/June, 47–58.

Fatas, A. (1997). EMU: Countries or regions? Lessons from the EMS experience. *European Economic Review, 41,* 743–751.

Fernández-Villaverde, J., & Krueger, D. (2002). *Consumption over the life cycle: Some facts from the consumer expenditure survey data* (NBER Working Paper 9382). http://www.nber.org/papers/w9382. Accessed 1 Dec 2014.

Giles, C. (2016, January 10). 35-year mortgages become the norm, Halifax figures show. FT.com.

Giussani, B., & Hadjimatheou, G. (1991). Modelling regional house prices. *Regional Science, 70,* 201–219.

Goodhart, C., & Hofmann, B. (2008). House prices, money, credit, and the macroeconomy. *Oxford Review of Economic Policy, 24*(1), 180–205.

Gray, D. (2012). District house price movements in England and Wales 1997–2007: An exploratory spatial data analysis approach. *Urban Studies, 49,* 1411–1434.

Gray, D. (2015). Are prices of new dwellings different? A spectral analysis of UK property vintages. *Cogent Economics and Finance, 3*(1), 1–16.

Gregoriou, A., Kontonikas, A., & Montagnoli, A. (2014). Aggregate and regional house price to earnings ratio dynamics in the UK. *Urban Studies, 51,* 2916–2927.

Hamnett, C. (1988). Regional variations in house prices inflation, 1969–1988. *The Royal Bank of Scotland Review, 159,* 29–40.

Ho, L., Ma, Y., & Haurin, D. (2008). House price changes across quality tiers. *Journal of Real Estate Finance & Economics, 37*(4), 299–316.

Holly, S., Pesaran, H., & Yamagata, T. (2011). The spatio-temporal diffusion of house prices in the UK. *Journal of Urban Economics, 69*(1), 2–23.

Holmes, M. (2007). How convergent are regional house prices in the United Kingdom? Some new evidence from panel data unit root testing. *Journal of Economic and Social Research, 9*(1), 1–17.

Holmes, M., & Grimes, A. (2008). Is there long-run convergence among regional house prices in the UK? *Urban Studies, 45*(8), 1531–1544.

Hui, H.-C. (2011). Cycles in landed and non-landed housing sub-markets in Malaysia. *International Journal of Housing Markets and Analysis, 4*(2), 144–154.

Iacoviello, M., & Pavan, M. (2013). Housing and debt over the life cycle and over the business cycle. *Journal of Monetary Economics, 60,* 221–238.

Jadevicius, A., & Huston, S. (2014). A "family of cycles"—major and auxiliary business cycles. *Journal of Property Investment & Finance, 32*(3), 306–323.

Jin, C., & Grissom, T. (2008). Forecasting dynamic investment timing under the cyclic behavior in real estate. *International Real Estate Review, 11*(2), 105–125.

Jones, C., & Leishman, C. (2006). Spatial dynamics of the housing market: An interurban perspective. *Urban Studies, 43*(7), 1041–1059.

Jones, C., Leishman, C., & Watkins, C. (2003). Structural change in a local urban housing market. *Environment and Planning A, 35,* 1315–1326.

JRF. (1995, November). *New regional household growth projections create challenges for regional housing and planning policies.* Joseph Rowntree Foundation Housing Research 161. https://www.jrf.org.uk/file/37464/download?token=oiM0VCDE. Accessed 4 Apr 2016.

Leamer, E. (2007). *Housing is the business cycle* (Working Paper 13428). NBER.

Leamer, E. (2015). Housing is the business cycle: What survives the lessons of 2008–09? *Journal of Money Credit and Banking, 47*(1), 43–50.

Lee, C.-C., & Chien, M.-S. (2011). Empirical modelling of regional house prices and the ripple effect. *Urban Studies, 48*(10), 2029–2047.

Lettau, M., & Ludvigson, S. (2004). Understanding trend and cycle in asset values: Reevaluating the wealth effect on consumption. *The American Economic Review, 94*(1), 276–299.

Levin, E., & Pryce, G. (2009). What determines the price elasticity of house supply? *Real Interest Rate Effects and Cyclical Asymmetries, Housing Studies, 24*(6), 713–736.

Li, W., & Yao, R. (2007). The life-cycle effects of house price changes. *Journal of Money, Credit and Banking, 39*(6), 1375–1409.

Liow, K. (2007). Cycles and common cycles in real estate markets. *International Journal of Managerial Finance, 3*(3), 287–305.

Luea, H. (2008). The impact of financial help and gifts on housing demand and cost burdens. *Contemporary Economic Policy, 26*(3), 420–432.

Luo, Z., Liu, C., & Picken, D. (2007). Housing price diffusion pattern of Australia's state capital cities. *International Journal of Strategic Property Management, 11*(4), 227–242.

Marchand, C. (1981). Maximum entropy spectra and the spatial and temporal dimensions of economic fluctuations in an urban system. *Geographical Analysis, 13,* 95–116.

Mayer, C., & Engelhardt, G. (1996). Gifts, down payments and housing affordability. *Journal of Housing Research, 7*(1), 59–75.

McDonald, J. (1985). Expectations and urban housing prices. *Urban Studies, 22,* 543–549.

McGough, T., & Tsolacos, S. (1995). Property cycles in the UK: An empirical investigation of the stylized facts. *Journal of Property Finance, 6*(4), 45–62.

Meen, G. (1998). Modelling sustainable home-ownership: Demographics or economics. *Urban Studies, 35*(11), 1919–1934.

Meen, G. (1999). Regional house prices and the ripple effect: A new interpretation. *Housing Studies, 14*(6), 733–753.

Meen, G. (2011). The economic consequences of mortgage debt. *Journal of Housing and the Build Environment, 26*(3), 263–276.

Montagnoli, A., & Nagayasu, J. (2015). UK house price convergence clubs and spillovers. *Journal of Housing Economics, 30,* 50–58.

Morrow-Jones, H., & Wenning, M. (2005). The housing ladder, the housing life-cycle and the housing life-course: Upward and downward movement among repeat home-buyers in a US metropolitan housing market. *Urban Studies, 42*(10), 1739–1754.

Munro, M., & Tu, Y. (1996). The dynamics of UK national and regional house prices. *Review of Urban and Regional Development Studies, 8*(2), 186–201.

Oikarinen, E. (2006). The diffusion of housing price movements from center to surrounding areas. *Journal of Housing Research, 15,* 3–28.

Ortalo-Magné, F., & Rady, S. (2006). Housing market dynamics: On the contribution of income shocks and credit constraints. *Review of Economic Studies, 73*(2), 459–485.

Peersman, G., & Pozzi, L. (2007, November). *Business cycle fluctuations and excess sensitivity of private consumption* (Bank of England Working Paper No. 335).

Pesaran, M. H. (2007). A pair-wise approach to testing for output and growth convergence. *Journal of Econometrics, 138,* 312–355.

Pollakowski, H., & Ray, T. (1997). Housing price diffusion patterns at different aggregation levels: An examination of housing market efficiency. *Journal of Housing Research, 8*(1), 107–124.

Pritchett, C. (1984). Forecasting the impact of real estate cycles on investment. *Real Estate Review, 13*(4), 85–89.

Pryce, G., & Sprigings, N. (2009). Outlook for UK housing and the implications for policy: Are we reaping what we have sown? *International Journal of Housing Markets and Analysis, 2*(2), 145–166.

Pugh, C., & Dehesh, A. (2001). Theory and explanation in international property cycles since 1980. *Property Management, 19*(4), 265–297.

Pyhrr, S., Roulac, S., & Born, W. (1999). Real estate cycles and their strategic implications for investors and portfolio managers in the global economy. *The Journal of Real Estate Research, 18*(1), 7–68.

Reed, R., & Wu, H. (2010). Understanding property cycles in a residential market. *Property Management, 28*(1), 33–46.

Rosenthal, L. (1986). Regional house price interactions in the UK, 1975–81: A cross-spectral analysis. *Applied Economics, 18,* 1011–1023.

Royal Institute of Chartered Surveyors (RICS). (1999). *UK Property Cycle—A History from 1921 to 1997.* London: RICS Books.

Sanidas, E. (2014). Four harmonic cycles explain and predict commodity currencies' wide long term fluctuations. *Technological Forecasting and Social Change, 87,* 135–151.

Scanlon, K., & Whitehead, C. (2011). The UK mortgage market: Responding to volatility. *Journal of Housing and the Build Environment, 26,* 277–293.

Schularick, M., & Taylor, A. (2012). Credit booms gone bust: Monetary policy, leverage cycles, and financial crises, 1870–2008. *American Economic Review, 102*(2), 1029–1061.

Sheiner, L. (1995). Housing prices and the savings of renters. *Journal of Urban Economics, 38*(1), 94–125.

Shi, S., Young, M., & Hargreaves, B. (2009). The ripple effect of local house price movements in New Zealand. *Journal of Property Research, 26*(1), 1–24.

Smith, B., & Tesarek, W. (1991). House prices and regional real estate cycles: Market adjustments in Houston. *Real Estate Economics, 19*(3), 396–416.

Smith, L., & Ho, M. (1996). The relative price differential between higher and lower priced homes. *Journal of Housing Economics, 5,* 1–17.

Sommervoll, D., Borgersen, T.-A., & Wennemo, T. (2010). Endogenous housing market cycles. *Journal of Banking & Finance, 34*(3), 557–567.

Spotton, B. (1997). Financial instability reconsidered: Orthodox theories verses historical facts. *Journal of Economic Literature, 31,* 175–195.

Stein, J. (1995). Prices and trading volume in the housing market: A model with down-payment effects. *The Quarterly Journal of Economics, 110,* 379–405.

Stevenson, S. (2004). House price diffusion and inter-regional and cross-border house price dynamics. *Journal of Property Research, 21*(4), 301–320.

Stevenson, S., Akimov, A., Hutson, E., & Krystalogianni, A. (2014). Concordance in global office market cycles. *Regional Studies, 48*(3), 456–470.

Sun, J., Sim, L.-L., Hin, K., & Ho, D. (2007). The cyclical association of residential housing price and consumption. *Journal of Real Estate Portfolio Management, 13*(3), 219–248.

Tsai, I.-C. (2014). Ripple effect in house prices and trading volume in the UK housing market: New viewpoint and evidence. *Economic Modelling, 40,* 68–75.

Tsai, I.-C. (2015). Spillover effect between the regional and the national housing markets in the UK. *Regional Studies, 49,* 1957–1976.

Tu, Y. (2000). Segmentation of Australian housing markets: 1989–98. *Journal of Property Research, 17*(5), 311–327.

Wilson, P., & Okunev, J. (1999). Spectral analysis of real estate and financial assets markets. *Journal of Property Investment and Finance, 17*(1), 61–74.

Wilson, P., & Zurbruegg, R. (2008). Big city difference? Another look at factors driving house prices. *Journal of Property Research, 25*(2), 157–177.

Wood, R. (2003). The information of regional house prices: Can they be used to improve national house price forecasts? *Bank of England Quarterly Bulletin, 43*(3), 304–314.

Worthington, A., & Higgs, H. (2003). Co-movements in UK regional property markets: A multivariate cointegration analysis. *Journal of Property Investment Finance, 21*(4), 326–347.

Wunder, T. (2012). Income distribution and consumption driven growth: How consumption behaviors of the top two income quintiles help to explain the economy. *Journal of Economic Issues, 46*(1), 173–192.

Wynne, M., & Koo, J. (2000). Business cycles under monetary union: A comparison of the EU and US. *Economica, 67,* 347–374.

Yang, Z., & Wang, S. (2012). Permanent and transitory shocks in owner-occupied housing: A common trend model of price dynamics. *Journal of Housing Economics, 21,* 336–346.

3

Housing Market Theory

Abstract In this chapter, the monocentric urban model due to DiPasquale and Wheaton (1996) is outlined with a view to explain how prices are maintained across an urban housing area. This is extended across space, buyers, and quality tiers. A discussion of cycles in economic variables in general and property in particular follows.

Keywords Housing market theory · Urban housing · Monocentric urban model

3.1 Introduction

The version of monocentric urban model due to DiPasquale and Wheaton (1996) is outlined with a view to explain how prices are maintained across an urban housing area. This is extended to space, buyers, and quality tiers. A discussion of cycles in economic variables in general and property in particular follows.

Different models of interaction are considered. In particular, Limtanakool et al.'s (2009) overarching framework of nodal

D. Gray, *Cycles in the UK Housing Economy*,
DOI 10.1007/978-3-319-63348-0_3

interdependence can encompass balanced and imbalanced regional economic models. As such, monocentric and polycentric urban perspectives can be captured.

3.2 Monocentric Urban Model

An approach to a monocentric urban model which recognises factor intensity problems but does not incorporate factor substitution into [much of] the analysis is presented by DiPasquale and Wheaton (1996). They aver that the supply of land sets the overall market price level, but it is a demand that determines relative property values, and it is here that attention should be focused when seeking to examine why the prices of land and property vary considerably within the same locale or market. The demand for property in a market is a function of the number of households, income, and the annual cost of owning property.

To explain relative property values, they consider the flow of utility or services that the house and its location provide. Each dwelling has a bundle of characteristics, each of which is assumed to be homogenous across properties, and can be priced. Workers commute a distance of d to a central business district (CBD) from their dwelling. The commuting cost both pecuniary and non-pecuniary involves the cost per unit k, which is assumed to be a linear function of distance. Rent $R(d) = Y - kd - C$, where household income Y is spent on accommodation or alternatively, C, other consumption goods. Assuming households have a common income and other expenditures, the choice of where to locate is based on rent and distance from the CBD. The premium for property at one location should reflect the present value of the utility from living there relative to other places. If housing rents do not offset commuting costs, e.g. there is spare expenditure capacity in the system, those who are willing to offer more for a closer location give up this surplus. This bids up rent closer to the CBD and lowers it further away. In other words, there are adjustments to ensure that housing rent in the interior of the city offsets the savings in commuting. Utility is the same wherever one locates.

As displayed in Fig. 3.1, this premium, in a simple, monocentric urban model with a central business district, reflects the disutility associated with commuting to the centre. There is an employment centre, and the areas that surround it are populated with residential dwelling units of size q. Beyond the circular residential space is the agricultural zone. Workers commute to the centre, generating a Ricardian rent. This involves relating the rent, $R(d)$, or lump sum that a worker is willing to pay to reduce or evade commuting to the employment centre and a commuting cost function k, which is assumed to be a linear function of distance. The extent of the city boundary is b_0. The closer one locates to the city centre, the greater the locational, and hence housing, rent. An expression that links rent with the above is $R(d) = r^a q + c + k(b_0 - d)$. The rent at the boundary b_0, which is the lowest in the city, is determined by annualised housing construction costs (c) plus agricultural rents per hectare (r^a), and q is the number of houses per hectare. The structural rent could be considered the annualised mortgage payments that would cover the rebuilding costs. To the west of this, Ricardian rents are paid to avoid the maximum commute. Here, d is measured from the city's edge. The disutility of commuting reflects the rent premium paid to avoid it.

If the wage is such that the rewards from working in the urban area are greater than elsewhere, there will be in-migration, an expansion of

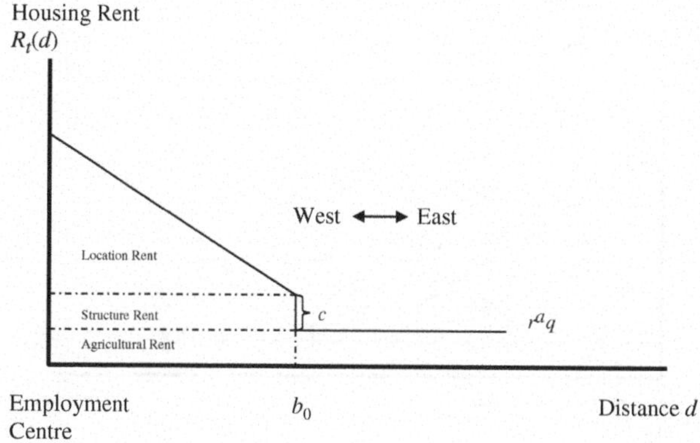

Fig. 3.1 Determinants of housing rents

the number of households, and a greater commuting shed. Agricultural land is drawn within the urban boundary, which extends outwards to b_t at time t in Fig. 3.2. An expression that links rent with the above at time t is $R_t(d) = r^a q + c + k(b_t - d)$. Rent has increased by $k(b_t - b_0)$ at b_0. The higher wage rate explains the willingness to undertake longer commutes.

If income for all households rises but construction is prohibited, the rent schedule for all housing is subject to the additional rent premium. In other words, rent absorbs the additional wage increase. In Fig. 3.3, the rent schedule for the initial household income is solid. The additional premium rent, the vertical distance between the solid and the dashed line, absorbs all the increase in income.

If there are two types of housing each of lot size q: good quality and poor quality, distributed evenly, the rents at any location $d < b_0$ will reflect this divide. In Fig. 3.3, the rent schedule for the good quality housing is subject to an additional premium rent, the vertical distance between the solid and the dashed line. One could relate this to the higher construction cost c^* or possibly housing maintenance or age. To compensate those who are willing to take on poor-quality housing, the rent is lower. Put another way, better quality accommodation is bid up in rent for every unit distance from the CBD relative to the poorer quality dwelling.

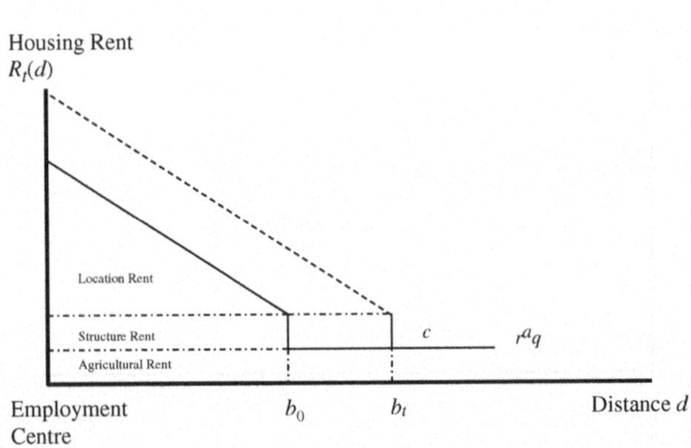

Fig. 3.2 Determinants of housing rents with a growing market

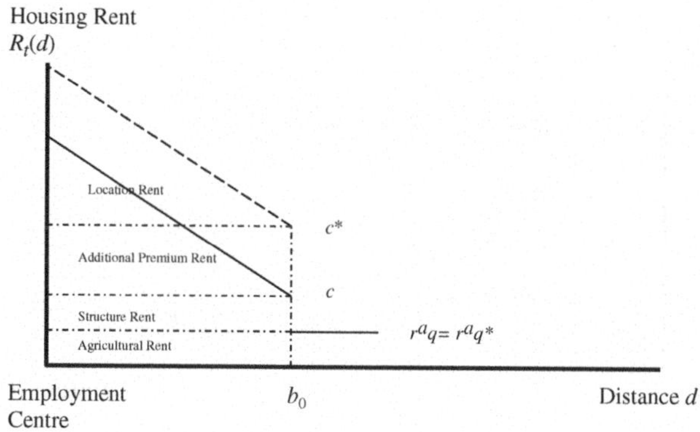

Fig. 3.3 The impact of dual housing markets on rents

If there are two types of housing each of lot size q and q^*: small and large, the rents at any location $d < b_0$ will reflect this divide. In Fig. 3.3, the rent schedule for the large housing is subject to a premium, the vertical distance between the solid and the dashed line. One could relate this to the greater construction cost c^* and the lower density accommodation q^*. The more modest accommodation could be viewed as part of a separate market, providing dwellings to those on lower incomes, who can afford a lower rent. Put another way, larger accommodation is bid up in rent for every unit distance from the CBD by those that value the space.

When two groups differ because of their dislike of commuting and hence have divergent commuting costs, the two groups will have differing levels of utility at any location $d < b_0$. Given the same income, the one that dislikes commuting more will outbid the second group across all space where commuting generates a positive utility from work: equilibrium is not possible.

Assume there is enough housing for both groups, the first group will outbid group two, opting for higher rents $R_1(d)$ up to point s. After this distance, the second group, willing to absorb greater commuting costs, will pay lower rents $R_2(d)$, as displayed in Fig. 3.4. This reflects a basic argument. Competition between groups generates segregation based on characteristics or preferences. Those living further afield have a higher consumption of non-housing services but face more time commuting.

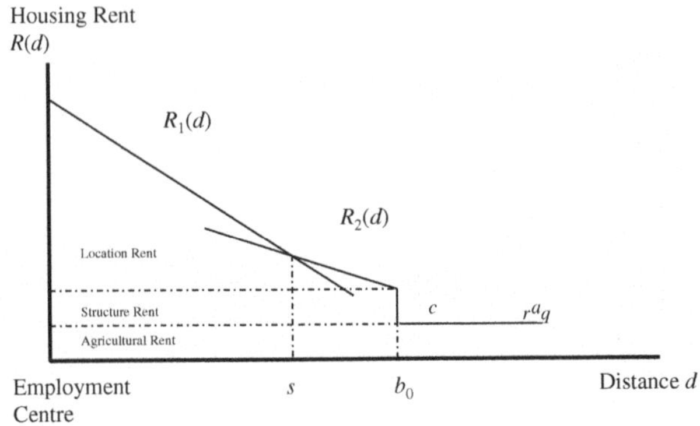

Fig. 3.4 Analysis of land allocation in a housing renting market

When two groups differ because of their income, as the higher income group would outbid the lower across all space, there is no equilibrium. To find an equilibrium, again we must treat the two groups differently. Using Fig. 3.4, if group 2 is more sensitive to lot size and is less worried by commuting costs, it will occupy the space further from the centre. It is suggested that higher income groups with families are likely to reflect the characteristics of group 2. DiPasquale and Wheaton (1996) argue that the outcome is dependent on the income elasticity of demand for land and price elasticity of demand for commuting.

Note that the land rent and the housing rent are related. Land is the residual from income-consumption and commuting. Ignoring building costs, a greater density of dwellings can increase the return to land. The housing rent per dwelling decreases, but the land rent per hectare can increase. It is likely that, as land has greater value/unit size closer to the CBD, it will be used more intensively, so that q varies directly with distance from the CBD. For low-income households to occupy spaces closer to the CBD that make commuting affordable, the landlord needs to offer accommodation that is affordable also. This implies multiple occupancy dwellings: low housing rent but high land rent. The type of dwelling must be unappealing to higher income households; otherwise, they will outbid the poor. A life cycle model of household demand would posit that space stress would lead to this type of dwelling becoming unappealing with an expanding nuclear family. This could correspond with rising incomes. Space becomes more desirable, encouraging the renter to seek other, larger dwellings further afield. This implies household churn.

The dynamics of city development mean that lower density dwellings at time 0 could be on the edge, but at time *t* be well inside the city limits. As the demand for particular space increases, 'rent' rises leading to incentives to change the housing stock in that space. The land could be used more intensively with a higher density of accommodation returning a higher rent per hectare. This includes turning larger houses into multi-occupancy flats and building taller properties. The redevelopment of a site at this radius may lead to a change in the density of dwelling depending on what is most profitable at the time. So, redevelopment is likely to lead to a change in the quality of housing and plot size.

3.3 Interaction of Urban Centres

DiPasquale and Wheaton note that their approach could apply equally to a continuum of towns as to a single city. Town replaces location in determining rent. Urban areas will have a greater density and smaller average unit size than rural areas. Despite the differences between housing areas, they can still be seen as part of the same housing market if there is a tendency towards a stable structure of rents.

The interaction of an Urban Centre and local Competing Centre can be seen in Fig. 3.5. Here, land rather than housing costs are analysed, so construction costs are ignored, and a standard unit dwelling size is assumed. Workers receive higher pecuniary and non-pecuniary rewards in the 'central business district' (CBD) than in the Competing [population] Centre. Within the CBD and the Competing Centre between d_5 to d_7 and d_2 to d_3, there is no commuting. From d_4 to d_5, workers commute to the CBD; from d_4 to d_3, workers commute to the Competing Centre. At d_4, workers are indifferent to working at either employment centre.

A variation of the Fig. 3.5 analysis indicates the codetermination of house rents across areas that are substitutes. A favourable shock to the CBD that renders the wage offered there to rise, increasing the

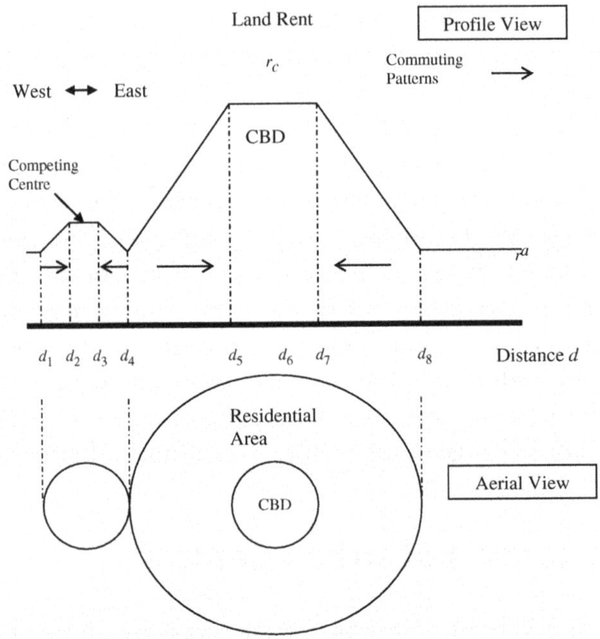

Fig. 3.5 Commuter flows between Urban Centres

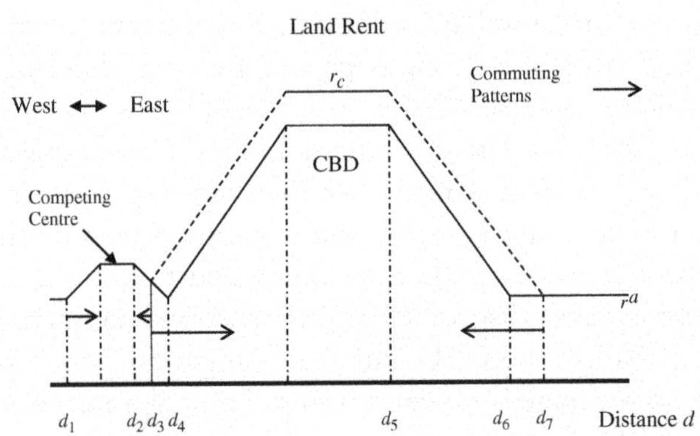

Fig. 3.6 Commuter flows between Urban Centres with income changes

compensation for commuting. Workers, who would commute to the CBD from as far out as d_6 in Fig. 3.6, will be willing to commute from d_7, which is further afield. This implies that the urban area expands.

The impact of the wage increase, between d_2 and d_3, will raise rents and encourage some to switch from commuting to the Competing Centre to the CBD. If the zones about which house rent data are collected remain d_4 to d_6 for the CBD and d_1 to d_4 for the Competing Centre, average house rents in both areas rise. Indeed, a change in conditions in one market has had an impact on a neighbouring, interlocked, substitute, housing market. This interlocking requires those commuting to one centre to be able to switch to another. On the east of the city, there is some immigration.

The rent and price gradients are presumed to be a negative linear function of distance from the centre to the outskirts of the city. It is unlikely the decline is smooth or linear. DiPasquale and Wheaton point out that around cities are zones or suburbs of high house rents. The impact is demonstrated in Fig. 3.7.

These inflated rents could reflect proximity to amenities, such as a good school, which would interact with the negative rent gradient associated with a monocentric model.

The interaction between an Urban Centre and local Competing Centre where there is a restriction on construction, such as in a green belt, and rents associated with suburbs can be seen in Fig. 3.8. The green belt extends round the urban area, constraining the residential population to live in the zone between d_4 and d_{10}. The green belt policy prohibits any building of property but does not prevent commuting between d_4

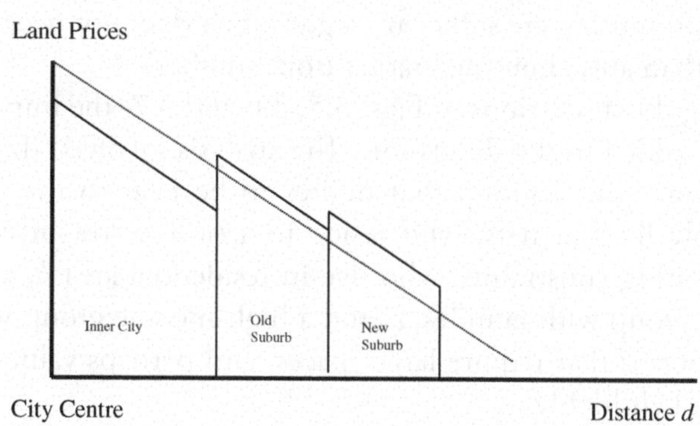

Fig. 3.7 Land prices and suburbs

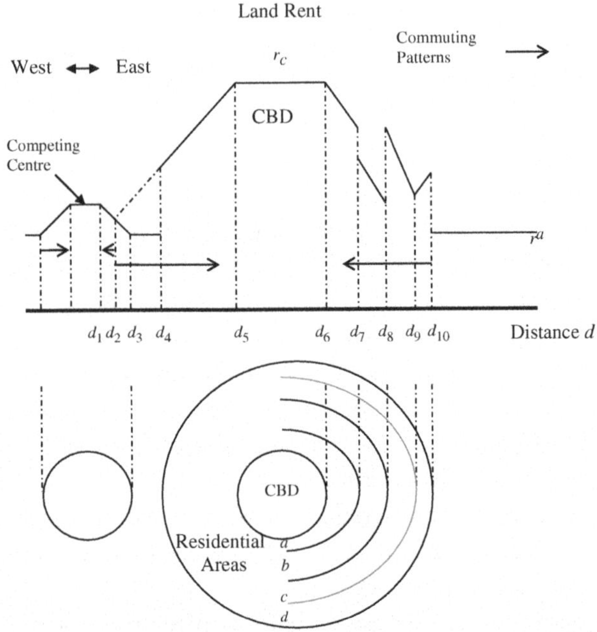

Fig. 3.8 Commuter flows between Urban Centres with suburbs and a green belt

and d_3. Net benefits are such that workers that reside in the Competing Centre on the other side of the green belt between d_2 and d_3 commute through the green belt to the CBD. At d_2, workers are indifferent to working at either employment centre. Thus, assuming that the net benefits from commuting are sufficient, a green belt does not necessarily segregate on urban area's housing market from another's.

Following the discussions of Figs. 3.5, 3.6 and 3.7, the impact of suburbs can be added to the discussion. The analysis involved three groups: a high-income young group that desires to be near to the city lights, and probably lives in flats, who reside in area *a*; a low-income group with commuting constraints, who live in residential area *b*; and a middle-income group with families, *c*, and a high-income group who live in residential area *d* that require large spaces, and perhaps value proximity to the green belt highly.

The rent gradient on the east of the urban area contains discontinuities that reflect suburbs and proximity to amenities. Still presuming that commuting is a bad, the distance from the CBD is a key determinant of rent. However, the model can be adapted to encompass good schools, shopping centres, lakes, etc. Here, house rents are greater at d_{10} than at d_9 despite the latter being closer to the CBD. This is possible if the commuter values the green belt more highly than the costs of commuting to the CBD. House rents are higher at d_8 than at d_7 reflecting the income groups that reside there. Indeed, the lumpy residential house rent market need not be continuous, so that rural zones could fall under the canopy of commuting without being contiguous with the Urban Centre.

3.4 From Rent to House Prices

In Fig. 3.9, house prices can be derived from the rent at time 0. With the demand for rented accommodation at q_1, the rent is R_0. Through the capitalisation of the present value of discounted rent R_0/i where i is the discount value, the price of a dwelling is P_0. This relationship can be altered to accommodate depreciation of the dwelling $\frac{R_0}{i+\delta}$ and if the dwelling is rented by an agent, agency costs $\frac{R_0(1-\omega)}{i+\delta}$, where ω is the proportion of the rent gone to managing the property and δ is the depreciation rate. As DiPasquale and Wheaton (1996) observe, the cost of capital for both the owner and the landlord should take into account

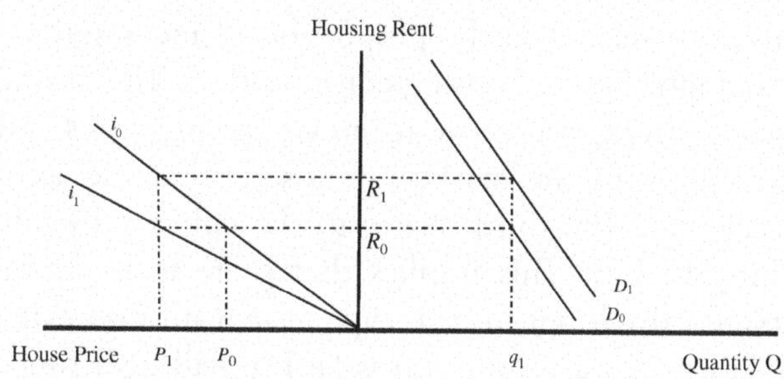

Fig. 3.9 House price-house rent

the expected appreciation of the capital or the present value of the asset when it is disposed.

An increase in the demand for rented accommodation, but with a fixed renting stock, boosts the demand by landlords to buy more dwelling, increasing the price they are willing to pay from P_0 to price P_1. Alternatively, assuming no change in the demand for accommodation, if the discount rate fell from i_0 to i_1, the cost of capital to the landlord would fall, lowering the rent needed for a given dwelling price. Correspondingly, this boosts the price a landlord is willing to pay for given the rent they could earn from P_0 to P_1.

Importantly, up to now, the presumption has been that the landlord is an absentee, earning Ricardian rent. However, the occupier of the dwelling could be the owner, acting as their own landlord. The rent could then be seen as the imputed rent from owning. The utility placed on renting and owning should be the same in a perfect housing market, with the household indifferent to either; otherwise, there is an arbitrage opportunity.

3.5 Buyers that are Sellers—A Key Source of Volatility

Stein (1995) analyses a housing market comprising only owner–occupiers wanting to buy. Due to rising equity in the dwelling, relaxed borrowing constraints particularly among repeat buyers of expensive housing can induce price volatility. He divides the impact of rising prices into three. The first is the unconstrained mover group, where the price of housing is related to the proportion of income that the owner is prepared to apportion to housing consumption. The second relates to those that switch from non-move to mover as price rises. Adding both demand and supply to the market, he asserts that the second impact is not an accelerant. The third relates to the enhanced equity of those already wishing to buy. This implies that there is an upward sloping demand curve for dwellings for this type of repeat buyer. Multiple equilibria would feature as a result, and volatility will be a function of the number of constrained relative to unconstrained buyers.

OMR provide a model of the relationship between first-time buyer (FTB) property prices and repeat buyers. Credit-constrained, owner–occupiers acquire more expensive 'houses', in the main, by selling their property once they have sufficient equity. In its most simple form, the housing ladder entails the FTB placing a down payment on a 'starter' home or 'flat', relying on an advance from a financial institution for the balance. An important implication of both Stein and OMR is that, as price increases their equity, the credit-constrained dwelling-mover has their budget constraint relaxed. In a period of rising prices, the windfall gain in equity is proportionally inversely related to the size of the original equity. As they are priced *in* rather than *out*, in a bubble, RBs' market participation lasts longer than FTBs. Moreover, as the RB can withdraw their property from the market in a downturn or offer them in an upturn with little time or cost they add turnover volatility to the markets when prices are already changing. OMR propose that steady state flat prices are proportional to FTB endowments, whereas steady state house prices rise less than proportionally with endowments but more in absolute terms than flat prices. One might expect that FTB participation in the housing market would be less volatile, driven perhaps by life events, such as starting a family, over which they may be some, but relatively little discretion over timing. OMR presumes that a purchase takes place when the flat can be afforded. However, with flat owners acting like bed-blockers, without RBs moving onto houses at the same rate as FTB wants to become flat owners, there may be raised flat price volatility. Benito (2006) notes that volatility in the OMR model can arise through fluctuations in income, particularly the marginal FTBs.

In Fig. 3.10, the scaling on both axes is the same so that the 45° line indicates the first-time buyer prices (for flats) are the same as repeat buyers (for houses). One could posit that in the long run, house prices are more expensive than flats by a factor of D reflecting the more sizeable plots etc. At time 0, the flat price faced by FTBs F_0 is less than the house price R_0. If the flat price rise to F_1, the accelerant inherent in Stein and OMR would, through a relaxed credit constraint, boost the house price to R_1. This is a short-run situation. The divide between the house and flat prices returns to a long-run situation at price R_2.

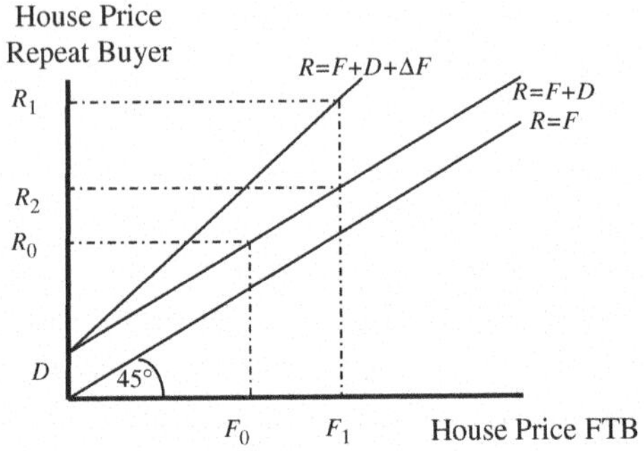

Fig. 3.10 RB–FTB ratio

Correspondingly, Stein's model has been applied to explain how expensive, highly geared houses are more volatile than cheaper (Smith and Ho 1996; Smith and Tesarek 1991). Logically, a rich node's housing market would be more volatile than a poorer, lower priced node. Stein's work implies leadership from high-price to lower priced regions, with the highest priced regions being the most volatile.

This brief visit to the monocentric urban model has shown that, among areas that are substitutable, commuters can switch between them but remain within the same housing market. Price and rent growth will be a function of [expected] population and income growth.

3.6 Shock and Cycle—Two Views

Van Duijn (1983) observes that cycles are an essential feature of the economic growth story. Virtually all aspects of economics life are cyclical. Waves or cycles are difficult to explain, and they call into question the assumption of a long-run unique equilibrium to which price is drawn. De Groot and Franses (2008) suggest there are two views on the presence of economic cycles. New Classical and New Keynesian business cycle theory, for example, do not even recognise the notion of a periodicity. These models posit that the fluctuations are based on shocks and reaction to shocks. Undulations are caused by shocks that are exogenous and are largely unpredictable, and are described here as the *shock* perspective. Mainstream economics conceptualises markets as essentially stable in nature with any shock that causes a deviation (in the short run) from the long-run steady state as temporary. Over time, through unfettered adjustments, the deviation or error will be corrected, and stability will be re-established. This long-run may not be achieved quickly or there may be additional shocks that move the system further from steady state. However, what is key in mainstream economics is the tendency towards equilibrium.

The alternative is that cycles are a permanent feature. De Groot and Franses argue that long-term economic stability comes from the persistence of multiple, robust cycles. They aver that, rather than exogenous shocks causing change and adjustment, it is the cycles that enable the system to absorb exogenous shocks that would otherwise put developed economies 'off balance'. This implies that (common) trends may alter, reflecting an exogenous shock, but cycles do not. The notion of a 'cycle' implies some sort of periodicity, but there tend to be irregular up-and-down movements in economic activity. They are not fully stochastic but partly deterministic. A cycle is identified as a sequence of four phases: trough, expansion, peak, and contraction. This is labelled the *cycle* perspective. Underlying that cycle is a trend. The trend could be measured from peak-to-peak or trough-to-trough.

House prices, output, and consumption have trends and are commonly diagnosed as being non-stationary. The workhorse for analysing such data is the ECM. It can capture common trends, as well as short run, deviations from trends. There is the tendency for the mean-revision process to maintain stable differentials in the long run. Here, there is a long-run equilibrium.

One could suggest that a business cycle time series X_t can be seen as comprising a growth or trend element g_t and a cyclical element x_t. If, as is likely, this trend is nonlinear, it too could be seen as cyclical in that it undulates so that what is viewed as a trend could be seen in part as a long cycle with an unknown turning point. An essential feature of this cycle analysis is a decomposition of trends and cycle. For this, the Hodrick-Prescott, Butterworth, and Christiano-Fitzgerald are a means of extraction. The filtered cyclical element x_t is trendless but has tendency overshoot zero.

3.6.1 New and Traditional Periodicities

Traditionally, four main cyclical periodicities have been identified (Van Duijn 1983). First, three- to five-year 'Kitchin' inventory cycles, which could fit a political cycle in the post-World War II era. The 6–11 year so-called Juglar or business cycle is the one most commonly understood as an economic cycle. The 'Kuznets' cycle of 15–25 year is associated with infrastructure investment. The 'Kondratieff' cycle of 50–60 years is sometimes discussed as long waves of development or eras.

Beyond these, other authors have proposed other mechanisms and periodicities. A key critic of financial deregulation, the endogeneity of financial cycles and crises is Minsky. Palley (2011) explains that Minsky postulates two cycles: a basic and a super-cycle. Agents become progressively more optimistic about future asset prices, taking on more risk. There is a relaxation of credit constraints, boosting the funds that a borrower can access, increasing the assets' prices. The optimism of borrowers and imprudence of lenders are mutually reinforcing. Initially, borrowers can afford the interest and capital repayments on the loan. The next phase involves borrowers just meeting the interest payments on the capital, and the cycle ends with borrowers relying on capital gains to meet their obligations, which may force them to sell when a payment is due.

Minksy's super-cycle entails an erosion of the structures and institutions that moderate lending (thwarting institutions). Palley (2010) observes a thirty-year super-cycle in the USA involving financial innovation, financial deregulation, and changed investor attitudes to risk. This overarches three business cycles (1981–1990, 1991–2001, and 2002–2009), each of which was 'marked' by a basic cycle in which borrowers and lenders took on increasingly more financial risk.

Leamer (2007) adapts the Minsky financial cycle into housing. Here, lending standards are loosened, and lenders become less prudent. Stage one entails fulfilling prudent loan criteria, such as house price to earnings metrics. Specifically, can the borrower meet the interest payments and repay the capital. Stage two involves lending to those that can meet the interest payments, but some latitude is granted over the loan. This would be seen in a relaxation of lending criteria such as loan-to-value

(LTV) and loan-to-income (LTI) ratios. Using perhaps a permanent income perspective, income in the future is expected to be higher so the lender can satisfy itself that the debt will be repaid. Alternatively, the house price is expected to rise, covering the loan, leaving some capital left over, so the lender will not be out of pocket. This allows the lender to switch buyers to interest-only mortgages without a repayment vehicle. Last or Ponzi financing stage allows borrowers that cannot quite service the debt. They are encouraged by the offer of teaser rates or mortgages of over 100% of the property value. In this period such poorly monitored products as the self-certified mortgage feature. Here, the borrower reports their income, which the lender takes on faith. Madsen's (2012) model is consistent with such buyer behaviour.

Leamer (2007, 2015) argues that housing cycles are business cycles [in the USA]. As with DiPasquale and Wheaton, house building starts are key to the explanation. Importantly, he notes that 6 of the 10 recessions considered are preceded by a fall in housing starts. Indeed, weaknesses in housing starts and consumer durables precede recessions by possibly 4–5 quarters, and business equipment, which coincides with recessions. Interestingly, inventories followed by consumer durables and housing starts, in total explain half of the weaknesses in activity before and during recessions.

Along with construction, jobs that are most cyclically sensitive are in the manufacturing of durables. A temporary fall would at some point lead to less production to re-establish normal levels. Stocks of houses and cars can be built up in periods of 'over' production that overhangs the recession extending the recovery. A permanent fall in the real rate shifts consumption away from the future leading the current level of production being too low. Leamer argues that the real rate of interest determines the replacement rate of durables. In a neo-classical world, the real rate of interest affects inter-temporal consumption demand. When the real rate is low the equilibrium stock of durables, such as housing and cars, is high. A temporary interest rate shock can provoke a realignment of expenditure. Expenditure on durables such as cars can be delayed so should be cyclical. A surge in consumer durables sales in one-quarter in effect brings them forward, displacing them from the following quarter. Deflation of durable asset prices leads to lower levels of production, even if the renting market is buoyant. Leamer proposes that this deflation is a significant problem in a recession. Durables and housing are complements, not only in the purchasing but they are both a function of interest rates/credit restrictions and one can be used to finance the other.

In keeping with this myopic house purchasing world, Madsen (2012) proposes a behavioural model of house prices, where real effects are ignored and decisions are made in nominal terms. He develops a repayment model. Demand drives short-term prices and supply, determines them in the long. Mortgage lenders restrict credit on the basis of what is affordable. This is then related to sustainability of mortgage repayments. After-tax incomes are related to nominal house price. Thus, house prices are determined by down payments, household disposable income, nominal interest payments, the principal repayment, financial liberalisation/innovation and the net flow of buyers. The supply of housing is determined by the long-run replacement cost of housing.

As well as a lack of understanding of anything other than simple maths, buyers have an unrealistic view of future prices. Initial payments are key. Both lenders and borrowers implicitly believe that house purchase will be easier once the initial payments are made. This has some appeal. Incomes of the young could be expected to rise over their life cycle and the principal is paid off steadily over a 25 year period. Money illusion features so that the inter-temporal consumption choice will favour current consumption in an inflationary era. Inflation in Madsen's model affects house prices through interest rates. Interest rate only mortgages should not induce greater mortgage allocation, but as Madsen notes, it did in OECD countries. Madsen's model does not have a price accelerator related to equity. Rather, equity can be viewed as reducing the mortgage cost. Madsen notes that expectations of future growth can only feed through to house prices if credit is made available.

Harrison (2005) using a cycle of 18 years predicted a property crash in 2010. The cycle is based on the repayment of an asset. With a 5% return, an asset will have repaid itself in 14.2 years. Without compounding, it would take a further 6 years. Harrison anticipates a 14-year property boom with a correction of 4 years, giving an 18-year cycle.

One can see long cycles within Meen's (2011) four phases in mortgage provision in the UK. Up to the early 1980s, there was rationing by the

Building Society cartel. In the second, from then to around 1990, markets were being liberalised. With credit liberalisation, buyers could borrow more funds for a given level of income (Campbell and Mankiw 1991; Muellbauer 2007). In this phase, Scanlon and Whitehead (2011) point to housing demand being fuelled by greater accessibility of mortgage finance and mortgage interest tax incentives. This though should be seen as a ratcheting effect, raising the average debt level. The third phase, up to the mid-1990s, is marked by the first great housing bubble bursting, particularly affecting the high-priced South East of England. The macroeconomic consequences were severe as there was a housing market-driven recession. The fourth phase, up to 2008 when the second great housing bubble burst, Scanlon and Whitehead (2011) highlight the accessing of greater amounts of mortgage funding from wholesale markets that was abundant at the time by such institutions as Northern Rock. This phase was characterised by an increased use of mortgage brokers, mortgage equity release, buy-to-let mortgages and lax lending practices.

Consistent with a Minskyan view of the aftermath of a bubble, one could extend Meen's phases to include a fifth, the current phase, which features tightened lending criteria such as the Bank of England's loan-to-income restriction and elevated down payments expected of buyers (Palley 2011), which adversely affects FTBs in particular.

3.6.2 Cycles in House Prices

Pyhrr et al. (1999) review a large body of literature on real estate markets, concluding that 'the real estate literature supports the theory that real estate markets are cyclical' (p. 23). A cycle [in property] is a reoccurrant but irregular fluctuation in a price or return. The literature review separates microeconomic cyclical studies that focus on metropolitan areas, from macroeconomic, which emphasises the regional and national levels. Brown (1984) argues the key to studying real estate cycles is to removal of trend and seasonal effects. He advocates the measurement of cycles using time series data. Pritchett (1984) posits that, despite a common national house price cycle, there are separate, non-coincident ones of distinct types of property. Property supply follows demand, with cycle turning points occurring when growth of the two are in opposite directions. New construction occurs when occupancy is below a long-run average and ceases when above. Rental growth rates correspond with occupancy rates.

3.6.3 Life Cycle Effects on Consumption and Housing Choices

Rather than supply of new dwellings causing price cycle, demand-led pricing fluctuations could also occur. A first-time buyer household is one joining the property-owning sector for the first time. Given wealth, income and credit constraints, the generally FTB is limited to the lower end of the housing quality hierarchy. This may constitute a match with need, constrained by income. Mismatches between expanding family housing requirements and dwelling characteristics cause housing stress, provoking a greater urge to migrate. Once the children have left the family home, to complete a life cycle, the household could trade down back into a flat (OMR), or into a bungalow. The buyer's age is an important indicator of their income, family unit and the relative value of their property (Morrow-Jones and Wenning 2005). Dicks (1989) postulates a system where there is a seven-year lag between moves that predicts broadly the 'right' number of repeat buyers in the market.

3.6.4 The Interweaving of Cycles

Leamer's thesis concerning business and housing cycles is based, in part, on the interweaving of asset and loans. Banks became linked to housing through their move into Building Societies' territory of the provider of mortgages. By 2008, in the UK the mortgage lending made up 68% of the banks' total lending. As mortgages become impaired or non-performing there is pressure to address bank balance sheets. Illiquid assets become difficult to value. This commonly leads to self and regulatory-enforced risk aversion. The 2006–2009 housing market collapse did not cause, but deepen the recession. Jorda et al. (2016) find that mortgage credit booms are more painful that non-mortgage credit recessions in being deeper and having longer recoveries. Indeed, in keeping with Leamer, they note the impact of housing investment having a key influence the extended recovery period.

Grover and Grover (2014) highlight that property is subject to waves rather than cycles and these are affected by speculation, so prone to higher volatility than other economic cycles. They too link the property cycle to credit, highlighting the desire to recycle savings and the underestimation of default risk. The construction of new dwellings has a multiplier effect on the economy affecting materials and labour demand. They note that there is an additional multiplier through general investment. However, there are implementation lags that spread-out the impacts over time.

Persaud (2016) argues that the linkage of house prices, consumption, and unemployment should be recognised as a cyclical problem. Lower income households are more exposed to a downturn, particularly as it is likely that when they purchased a property the pushed the envelope of their constrained resources harder at the buying point.

3.6.5 Cycles and Expectations

Dusansky and Wilson (1993) highlight a duality in housing: houses have both consumption and investment dimensions. Owners of this good will form expectations about future price movements, opening up the possibility of an upward sloping demand curve for housing as the hope of capital gains outweighs the consumption role. These expectations of future capital gains are likely to be formed on the basis of past price increases, not future income streams (Clayton 1998; McDonald 1985; Spotton 1997). Consumption modelling also has this form of price determination. In Friedman's PIH in its original form, he presumed adaptive expectations.

Whilst exploring the role of expectations, DiPasquale and Wheaton put forward models of cyclical house prices. The three models are typified as exogenous, myopic and rational expectations. For both exogenous and rational expectations models, house price cycles can occur if other exogenous variables are subject to reoccurring changes, but should peter out without such perturbations.

With the adaptive expectations, a positive house price shock in period one is followed by price rises in subsequent periods building one on another. Additional construction work should be induced. However, the lag between housing starts and finishes allows prices to rise considerably. Eventually, this additional housing supply puts downward pressure on inflation, but the amount of new build is too great causing, in most cases, turning points (or bursting bubbles) in house price inflation. Moreover, as forecasts are adaptive, the fall in house prices is reinforced by negative future expectations, leading to a dramatic cut in new build. Thus, this model generates price cycles without an exogenous variable that is subject to reoccurring changes.

Sommervoll et al. (2010) generate price cycles from a simulation that is based on a series of single sealed bid auctions. The model allows for the expected price to be based on future prices so the duality highlighted by Dusansky and Wilson is incorporated. However, there is a maximum budget share that someone could apportion to servicing a mortgage, which places a cap on prices, and hence expectations. New builds and new buyers enter each subsequent auction. Sommervoll et al., project that the cycle length is a function of the updating of expectations, which are determined on an adaptive basis. Two base models are generated. With no equity, the amplitude or volatility is a function of the difference between the investment and the consumption motives, or the time preference for consumption. An increased average amount of equity a buyer might have lowers the frequency and amplitude.

The base models are used to explore credit rationing. Against the first model, the third simulation has a few cycles but then there is a price collapse. Compared with the second with equity model, the fourth projection also with equity has milder fluctuations compared with the third and also less frequent collapses.

Sommervoll et al. also subdivide the market into 'flats' and 'houses'. In their fifth simulation, all flat owners seek to buy a house each period. They find the cycles are synchronised, with flats more volatile than houses. However, the downturn in flat prices leads to an amplified collapse in houses. A sixth version with additional endowment other than equity in the flat suggests a reduced volatility in house prices in both absolute terms and relative to flats. As cycles are predicted with adaptive price expectations and without construction-determined turning points, this model has some useful characteristics for a UK environment.

3.7 Explanations of Inter-urban Price Co-movement

So far there has been a consideration of housing within an urban boundary, with rents and prices linked by a common income. DiPasquale and Wheaton's (1996) approach to house price differences across large expanses of terrain is based on local economic performance determined by distinct export and industrial structures. This income will vary over space and time. Thus, forces acting on demand in a property market will be a function of the nature of the urban system and the industries it hosts (Brühl and Lizieri 1994; Marchand 1981). A regional export base model (Armstrong and Taylor 2000) projects the performance of exports in determining income. By implication, the income will be a function of the exporting industries. The performance of these will be a function of the income of the trading partners. The more export-oriented the region, the more its income will be linked to external business cycles.

3.7.1 Balanced Economy Models

Within a balanced economies model, the primary driver behind economic activity is a territory's own economy. As such, a region can be viewed as a medium-sized nation within a single currency, open trading, multi-country system. In a balanced world, there are no systemic forces driving the system towards inequality. There is a wealth of literature on inter-country overspill and co-movement, which should be applicable to regions and cities.

A key conceptualisation of a region but in an 'international' context is the common currency area (CCA). In his seminal work on optimal currency areas, Mundell (1961) considers two nations with an identical industrial mix. Each country had specialised in two sets of industries that were located in two regions. For policy purposes, each region of a nation should react to *common* shocks in the same way, or absorb a regional specific (asymmetric) shock across both regions. Mundell points out that relative factor mobility defines the region. Mechanisms for absorbing an adverse asymmetric shock are located in the labour market. Wages should adjust downwards in, or there is outmigration from, the adversely affected region. The lower wages should reprice the exports making them more competitive. Alternatively, outmigration from the adversely affected would lower the unemployment problem and reduce wage pressures in the non-adversely affected region. Both wages and migration affect house rents and prices. As such, house prices should reflect this adjustment process.

If the labour markets are not that flexible, the two nations should be re-configured so that each country contained two regions with the same industrial structure so that the regional cycles would be the same.

Artis et al. (2011) posit that a small number of latent factors are common to international business cycles. The emphasis on synchronised business cycles of member countries is so that within functioning CCA policy initiatives do not destabilise a region. Incorporating countries with unsynchronised business cycles, De Grauwe (2003) notes, generates a less attractive feature of a CCA. Interest rate policy is problematic for a smaller country. Its reaction to a recession, to lower rates, is restricted and money supply contracts worsening the downturn. The money contraction is due to outflows to the larger country. This intensifies the smaller country's business cycle. De Grauwe describes this asynchronisation as asymmetric shocks.

Artis (2006) notes that there are two explanations for the 'convergence' of business cycles. The first concerns the intensification of international trade, exposing countries to common shocks or cycles. Krugman highlights the paradox that trade intensification will lead to increase specialisation and so distinctive industrial cycles. Regions have a tendency to specialise in a narrower range of goods and services than nations. Fatas (1997) suggests that distinct regional cycles are the consequence of two factors: first, specialisation and exposure to asymmetric, industry-specific shocks; and second, differences in sensitivity to economic policy initiatives.

Intra-industry trade theories highlight the 'same' goods traverse borders. The demand cycle of a class of goods would influence the home and the exporting country. Moreover, intermediate and final product industries would be linked to the demand for the final good. If those industries are located across countries, this would lead to more similar cycles. Thus, the production functions of associated countries would be co-dependent and some sort of international input–output model would be required when predicting national output. This proposition implies that, particularly with major firms working on regional rather than local markets, countries are linked through both production networks and consumption functions. Trade intensification implies enhanced export orientation and so stronger bonds between CCA countries. This proposition places trade at the heart of income synchronisation.

A portfolio approach to asset management links liquid stock exchanges around the globe so that adverse news in one market can overspill to another. Sentiment in the US, through the New York stock exchange, could be transferred overnight to the London stock exchange. Portfolios diversified across different country markets should increase the synchronisation of investment returns and income across countries.

Artis's second concerns convergence of administration so that policy-induced asymmetric shocks errors are less likely. Monetary integration enhances cycle synchronisation. Changes in a common interest rate act as common shocks to the system. Where there are differing currencies, the shock transmission is greater the more rigid the exchange rate.

Fiscal policy, when implemented counter-cyclically to dampen the business cycle, will be, in part, focused on the asynchronisations of output fluctuations. This may be related to countering the adverse effects of a common monetary policy. However, fiscal policy may not be implemented counter-cyclically. National fiscal multipliers are relatively low when the respective economies are open. Fiscal spillovers would affect both income and imports, which implies that the exporting country would also respond to the stimulus in the same direction, suggesting that fiscal overspill would enhance common movements. Germany's fiscal interventions, being a dominant European economy, would have a profound impact on, say, Slovakia.

Spatial consumption smoothing as a target does not require the synchronisation of business cycles. A central fiscal budget smooths consumption by reducing the tax burden on, and increasing the benefits to, the adversely affected region. De Grauwe is keen to emphasise that fiscal transfers between regions cannot be a permanent feature of a CCA. This implies that any regional divergence not met be labour market adjustment should be cyclical in nature. Secular trends imply some other form of intervention.

3.7.2 Urban Systems, Nodality and Imbalanced Economy Models

A national urban system comprises a hierarchy of cities or nodes, arranged by size and function. The number of centres and their populations is inversely related. Within the national system are regional subsystems that, again, are made up of cities but also towns, also arranged in some hierarchy. Storper and Walker (1989) identify three treads of this notion. With central place theory, there is a hierarchy of nodes or Urban Centres associated with both size and function. Second, the city's function reflects the roles placed upon it by large companies, under the banner of the new spatial division of labour. Third, Pred (1966) and Partridge et al. (2009) utilise the notions of cumulative causation and core-periphery to explain a hierarchy of function, activity and growth. Partridge et al. (2009) consider the urban hierarchy in the light of the New Economic Geography. A node with significant agglomeration economies extends a market for exports, potential workers and job opportunities to other nodes. Central place theory posits that the larger node offers higher level services. The New Economic Geography implies a (negative) shadow is cast over the neighbour; the neighbour could be at a cost disadvantage in a sector where spatial competition operates. Storper and Walker (1989) offer their own analysis of the city rank-size thesis, using the concept of propulsive industries, which has similarities with the New Economic Geography variant.

Duranton and Puga (2005) extend urban system theory to encompass business functions. In a world where business functions are disintegrated across space, higher level business services can become clustered in cities where companies locate their headquarters. Such services are best delivered on a face-to-face basis, so facilitating clustering. With globalisation, the theories have been extended to link (global) cities across borders (Godfrey and Zhou 1999; Derudder et al. 2003). London has distinctive cycles (Montagnoli and Nagayasu 2015), possibly as a result of it being linked into a global financial system (Fernandez et al. 2016; Holly et al. 2011). This provides further international ties beyond trade.

The pinnacle of a national urban system could be a single metropolitan area. As with a Russian doll, a lower order system is set within the regional. A daily urban system represents the 'life space' of urban residents (Herbert and Thomas 1995). In the UK national system, London holds the mantle of the city at the top of the hierarchy of cities, with the greatest number of headquarters and the largest sector supporting them in terms of legal and financial services. It is the largest city by some margin. Its commuter belt is the most extensive in the UK with the most comprehensive infrastructure to support it. It contains the boroughs with the highest house prices. London is linked to the second tier cities such as Leeds-Bradford (Yorkshire-Humberside), Manchester (North West) and Birmingham (West Midlands) via superior quality infrastructure, such as motorways and swift rail links. Third order metropolitan areas would be Liverpool (North West), Sheffield (Yorkshire-Humberside) and Newcastle (North) (McCann 2001). Higgins' (1983) work suggests that metropolitan areas behave symbiotically, interacting strongly. Olfert and Stabler (1999) find that the chief beneficiary of autonomous spending in a system is the nodal centre.

In a dual economy, agglomeration economies are accrued by the node or core and, through the migration of factors, innovation or cost advantages in trade, have both centripetal and centrifugal consequences for the non-core area. The former involves denuding the non-core or periphery of its productive capacity, whilst the latter relates to the spreading of economic activity from the centre to the periphery (Myrdal 1957; Perroux 1950). Some authors present the periphery as being dominated, or controlled by, a relatively autonomous, agglomerated core in an urban hierarchy (Richardson 1978, p. 151). Models that describe the characteristic spatial inequality and imbalanced growth of capitalist systems, entailing systemic approaches to spatio-temporal interactions between regions on hierarchical and connectivity bases, including core-periphery, have been presented by Friedmann (1973), Hirschman (1958), Krugman (1991), McCombie (1988), Myrdal (1957), Perroux (1950), Scott (1998), Storper (1995; 1997), and Storper and Walker (1989). The periphery can be viewed as being dominated or controlled by a relatively autonomous agglomerated core. Peripheral regions provide resources to the core suggesting that they should be better linked, both physically and metaphysically, to it than to other (non-neighbouring) peripheral regions. Moreover, the periphery's growth will be constrained by that of the core (McCombie 1988). However, Terluin (2003) finds that models involving networks of agents (such as Scott 1998; Storper 1995, 1997) with less of a power relationship better reflect economic development in rural areas than balanced or other unbalanced growth models.

De Grauwe (2003) discusses the notion of [productivity] growth differences among CCA members. Concentrating on income elasticities, he argues that fast-growing regions will not face a balance of payments constraint on growth. By contrast, Thirlwall's balance of payments constraint hypothesis (McCombie 1988) implies that the slower growing regions are constrained by the faster ones. As exports grow at a rate determined by their income elasticities and the income growth rate of the importing countries, De Grauwe's position is that the import elasticities are similar, avoiding a payments constraint. Thirlwall argues the poor region has an adverse constellation of elasticities, restricting its growth rate. In Krugman (1991) type models, the periphery is associated with agricultural produce whereas in McCombie (1988) they can produce staple manufactured goods but with low-income elasticities.

3.8 What is a Geographical Housing Market?

Despite differences in local property prices, DiPasquale and Wheaton argue that the structure of prices is stable over time, reflecting characteristics of the assets, including their location, which changes slowly. The stability of relative prices is based on arbitrage. In an efficient market sense, through mobility within a housing market, short-term changes in relative prices that constitute a mispricing of an asset should be eroded quickly. Properties with similar characteristics that occupy substitute locations are within a market: prices in one area do not move independently of those in another in the same market. If the house characteristics or the value or utility placed on them changes, such as with a dwelling extension, so does the property's relative price. If the locational attributes common to many houses change, such as the improvement in the local school, they are all affected. Arbitrage is central to the definition of a housing market. DiPasquale and Wheaton state that a housing market should encompass real estate parcels that are influenced by the same economic conditions. Practically, markets are delineated around labour markets and the willingness to commute. The substitutability of properties within a real estate market is derived from workers being able to change abodes without changing jobs, and switching jobs without moving home.

The monocentric model discussions in Sects. 3.2, 3.3, 3.4 and 3.5 explain that house price spillovers from one sub-market to another within the commuting canopy or shed via the bidding process for accommodation among different groups. Within the city boundary, a shock to one area will have an impact on prices in other areas of a real estate market as workers adjust their demand for substitute property locations. This applies to distinct qualities of dwellings at the same location.

A rise in household income or correspondingly the wage at the CBD has two outcomes: first, it attracts in-migration to the city; second, it allows existing residents to afford accommodation closer to the centre. The outcome for both is that the rent is bid upwards. If the stock of dwellings does not alter, the rise in population due to in-migration cannot be accommodated.

Where there are two households groups, the rise in income may not be common, perhaps favouring the richer group. There may be no net migration but a change in the proportion of high-income households. This then allows for some displacement of those that become better off less quickly (the relatively less well off). In the short run, the stock and quality of dwellings are fixed. As the relatively rich outbid others, this will force others to compete for accommodation in smaller dwellings, poorer quality dwellings or in lower cost urban area.

A lower interest rate boosts house prices relative to rents as does an increase in the lending metrics that mortgage providers use for assessing loans. This should encourage more to seek to own.

DiPasquale and Wheaton's approach to house price differences across large expanses of terrain, beyond the commuting shed is based on local economic performance determined by distinct export and industrial structures but *do not* discuss interactions. Both Wood (2003) and Meen (1999) consider a number of explanations for the house price ripple effect in the UK (at the regional level) that apply in the longer run. The first entails those that are shifting up the housing ladder, perhaps on a limited budget, looking beyond the local housing market area, forcing up prices within the search belt of neighbouring, substitute areas.

Second, Wood and Meen point to migrating to take advantage of differences in house prices as a mechanism for house price growth overspill. A third explanation entails expectations and spatial arbitrage, where financial, rather than physical flows, influence prices. Expectations of higher prices may encourage homeowners in one region could revise their asking (expected) price upwards. Meen's (1999) last explanation does not involve space. Instead, when regressors follow a similar configuration, spatial patterns in the determination of house prices can occur without spatial links. In other words, if the determinants of local house prices are the same across space and, say, income increases in all regions at broadly the same rate but with an ordered time lag, markets behave in the same way, then so, perhaps, should house prices.

DiPasquale and Wheaton's intra-urban pricing model relies on switching search behaviour. Disequilibrium is eroded swiftly through adjusting commuting expectations and bidding up prices in underpriced individual or groups of dwellings. This includes switching dwellings to reduce commuting time. Three Wood-Meen explanations rely on [potential] migration to maintain regional house price differentials so migration can be viewed as an intra- and inter-urban area equilibrating force (Jones and Leishman 2006). As migration is a weaker equilibrating force between urban areas than within them, price disequilibrium is resolved more slowly nationally and regionally than locally. So, the adjustment period back to spatial equilibrium is quicker where commuting is practical.

Meen's (1999) last, and preferred explanation is based on the similarly of the determinants of local house prices. Meen concludes that the dynamics of spatial differentials have little to do with cross-border migration. Rather, internal adjustments explain house price differences. If, as he argues, differences in regional economic growth explain variations in house prices, he is not relying on the existence of some sort of pressure-relieving mechanism that favours price transfer from high to low-priced regions.

Unlike DiPasquale and Wheaton, with the Meen-Wood ripple explanations there is no notion of hierarchy or core-periphery and yet these feature strongly in spatial economics. In regional system models, such as cumulative causation or urban systems theory, dominant nodes drive activity in the periphery. One might expect price dispersion to reflect a hierarchy and ripple effect explanations to incorporate such perspectives. Meen argues that the ripple effect could be explained by a common variable affecting local markets unrelated to house price overspill. For a ripple, rather than just diffusion, there must be some orderly delay across space: those regions closer to the driver must respond earlier than those further away.

DiPasquale and Wheaton's model is versatile. It presumes that a higher wage at the Urban Centre is a result of agglomeration economies. Larger centres have greater economies, pay higher wages and rents. The dual housing system in DiPasquale and Wheaton can be applied to imbalanced models, such as urban systems theory or cumulative causation. The core can be seen as the equivalent of the CBD plus the residential area in Fig. 3.5. The periphery could be those areas outside, including competing urban areas. The core to the system is likely to have a high labour concentration, the highest house prices, wages, commuting costs and largest commuting canopy, possibly overshadowing the markets of local areas. Unattractive and low wealth-generating areas are expected to exhibit low house prices.

The largest node, the one highest in the national hierarchy, could be a core area of the whole economy. Smaller nodes, with lower wealth-generating capacity, will be surrounded by a distribution of rich and not so rich areas in a similar vein. The land usage will not be as intense and house prices will be lower. Poor, lower level nodes and their hinterlands could form a periphery. Thus, it is anticipated that London will have a large commuter area/hinterland with high house prices. Birmingham and Manchester might be Competing Centres. Rural, poor areas and smaller towns would constitute a periphery.

Alternatively, analysis the model can accommodate edge or polycentric cities (Bogart 1998) and towns. Here, the differences in size make the power relations more equal. This will be more consistent with a balanced economy model.

3.8.1 A Unifying Framework to Consider Spatial Market Interaction

One could envisage a range of inter-urban/inter-country relationships. Limtanakool et al. (2007) and Limtanakool et al. (2009) develop a typology of urban systems involving dominant and non-dominant nodes. Their archetypes vary from a polycentric system to a full monocentric structure. Instead of triangular presentations seen in Limtanakool et al. (2007, p. 2127) and De Goei et al. (2010, p. 1159) the archetypal interaction between nodes can be explored in Fig. 3.11. The arrows indicate the direction of interaction with their thickness and continuity signifying the strength. A circle signifies a node, with its diameter indicating its importance. Each element could be varied to produce a range of interaction. An urban system with node A at its heart would entail

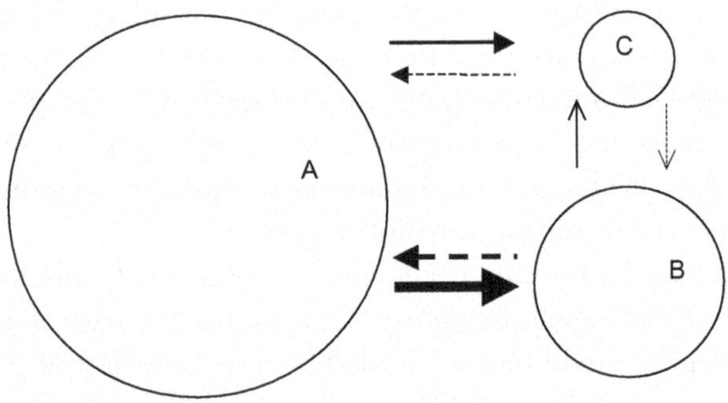

Fig. 3.11 Archetypal networks

a stronger link to second tier node B than to third tier node C. One way of viewing this is in terms of commuting and income. There could be a net commuting from B to A so that the gross income of node B would be partly dependent on the wealth generated in A. With a non-hierarchical, polycentric system, A, B, C would be of the same size and interact with each other on a balanced basis. Here, although no notable net flows, the gross commuting can vary so that the three nodes could be essentially one or 3 independents. Somewhere in between is a hierarchical system where A strongly affects node B and node B affects C likewise.

Figure 3.12 is a simple three-tier hierarchy with a dominant node (A), a city (E) and towns (B, C, D), laid out east-west to consider the nature of spatial interaction. In addition to the nodes, there are a road linking all five; a railway, connecting the cities; and a dashed oval representing the realistic extent of commuting. The spaces in between the nodes would be voids or [sparsely] populated rural areas. The dominant node's housing market envelops towns B, C and D. City E envelopes town D only. These images are consistent with Ali et al. (2011) who explore urban-rural links. Someone living in town D could work there or commute to city A or E or to town C. Because of the more modest wages and communications, the rewards from commuting beyond the neighbouring town are assumed to be insufficient to justify the journey costs.

A monocentric structure would be characterised by all other nodes being influenced strongly by the predominant centre. At the other extreme, a polycentric structure would have nodes interacting equally with each other. In between, the more likely arrangement is where the

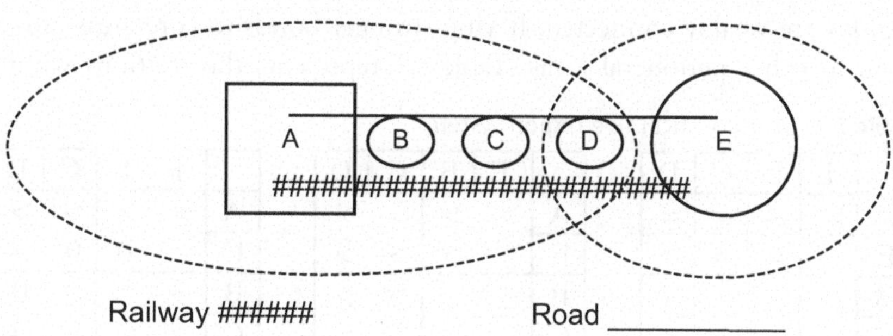

Fig. 3.12 Urban housing rents and interaction

higher-tier nodes (A & E) interact more strongly than the lower tier towns. Figure 3.12 could reflect a national and a regional urban system. City E could dominate a regional system (exemplified by town D). City A could dominate the region encompassing B, and C but also influencing town D. The superior infrastructure between the cities, represented by the rail connection, could make commuting between the cities feasible, linking their housing markets.

Inter-urban trade should influence activity within major cities. Increasing returns should generate some sort of a multiplier effect, so that the higher-order growth pole 'amplifies' additional demand, grows more rapidly, boosting activity in the rest of the system. Higgins' (1983) work suggests that metropolitan areas behave symbiotically, interacting strongly with others, possibly all over the world. However, the primary Urban Centre of the system should exhibit the largest impact of all, as Olfert and Stabler (1999) find. The extent to which this organises local activity depends on the degree of integration of those areas within the system. Where these cities are strongly linked, it is possible that, an impulse from City A affects City E more vigorously and/or more quickly than town B. Town B could affect C as before but E affects town D. This conjecture reflects work by Pred (1980) who finds greater city-to-city interaction compared with city and hinterland was evident from an early stage in USA development.

Borgatti and Everett (1999) present a framework for the modelling of core/periphery structures using directional linkages. This is adapted below to incorporate Limtanakool et al. (2007, 2009). Borgatti and Everett posit that core regions are strongly linked to each other whereas peripheral regions are weakly connected, having stronger bonds to core areas rather than to other peripheral areas. Table 3.1 represents the relations within

Table 3.1 A theoretical five-region system

	E	B	C	D
A	=	=	=	=
E		=	=	=
B			=	=
C				=

Table 3.1a

	E	B	C	D
A	>	>	>	>
E		>	>	>
B			>	>
C				>

Table 3.1b

	E	B	C	D
A	>	>	>	>
E		0	0	>
B			0	0
C				0

Table 3.1c

a theoretical five-territory system. This could be applied to an urban, a regional or national system of territories or nodes. Interaction between a pair of territories is indicated by coordinate a_{ij}. A balanced relationship is indicated by =. This implies the territories trade very much as equals in power terms, consistent with the balanced economy discussion. A power relation such as territory being higher in a hierarchy is indicated by >. So that A > B > C would indicate that territory A would have stronger influence on B than the obverse, and B would be correspondingly the dominant partner in flows with C, consistent with a core-periphery or hierarchy of nodes. Where there is no notable link, it is indicated by 0.

In Table 3.1a, all inter-territory trade is on a non-hierarchical basis, consistent with a polycentric urban system or a balanced trading system. One would anticipate that fluctuations (cycles) or shocks (trends) are passed from one territory to another. Territorial economic performance will be a function of the industrial structures. Following an export base model, incomes of territories will be linked.

Table 3.1b represents the relations within a theoretical five-territory hierarchal system. Territory A is higher up and has an asymmetric trading relation with B which is superior to C etc. The model implied in Table 3.1b is more coherent with a nodal system where the linkages are determined by the order properties of the sites (Bennett et al. 1985).

The model implied in Table 3.1c is more coherent with a core/leading and periphery system. Although territories B, C and D in Table 3.1c are linked to territory A they do not interact directly. The peripheral ones are codetermined through their leader-follower with A. Burns (1987) examines density of links to identify the degree of spatial integration of US states. He subdivides the spatial areas into 'core', 'integrated periphery', and 'unintegrated periphery'. Not only does Burns emphasise trade as a key link between regions, but also stresses the income elasticity characteristics of the region's export product mix as a major determinant of differential growth.

Meen's (1999) last explanation would view each region as isolated, so the regional dwelling dynamics would not be based on interaction horizontally (looking for a similar dwelling in a different region). The ripple would reflect the co-movements of regional business cycles. Alternatively, drawing from currency area assessments, DiPasquale and Wheaton's inter-urban proposition and export base models, regional cycle co-movements reflect income codetermination due to inter-regional trade arrangements.

London should lead East Anglia, as it is part of its commuting shed. On a hierarchy basis, as their cities there are lower tier ones, London should lead the East Midlands and Yorkshire-Humberside. The East Midland, between London and Yorkshire-Humberside, should lag its northern neighbour as it accommodates lower tier cities, such as Nottingham. One a ripple basis, as it is close to London, it should lead its northern neighbour. The North East is further away from London than other regions mentioned and Newcastle is a lower/smaller city. Thus, the North East should follow under both the ripple and hierarchical models.

Neither does the Meen-Wood description consider the FTB–RB nexus. A rise in flat prices in a high-price region will disfavour the FTB. They switch their search towards less expensive flats further from the relevant CBD, perhaps in an associated neighbouring lower-price region.

A rise in house prices in the high-price region will give the RB more collateral. When trading up, by searching in both the high and low-cost region, with enhanced equity, the RB find more within reach in the short run. However, by shifting to searching in the low-cost region, at the expense of greater commuting, the RB would be bidding up prices and adding volatility in the low-cost region.

A rise in house prices in the low-price region will give the RB more collateral, but price out the marginal FTB. The RB could trade-up locally, searching for a better quality dwelling. However, the RB could search for a similar dwelling in the high-price region, perhaps reducing commuting costs.

Meen's second ripple explanation focuses on the RB. Migrating to take advantage of price differentials would place downward price pressure on the high cost and upward pressures in the low-cost region. Here, spatial arbitragers might be moving 'horizontally', narrowing the house price differential across the two regions. Alternatively, this could capture those in the latter phase of their life cycle, trading down from a house to a flat and extracting more equity. House, not flat prices are diffused across the two regions. Where there are multiple regions no spatial pattern from this form of diffusion posited.

The third explanation, the upward revision of asking prices, would apply to the selling price of RB's flats and houses. Prices can move from one equilibrium level to another without a temporary increase in transactions. If the [expected] inflow was to occur in the low-cost region, the house and flat owners would see an instant equity increase, favouring the selling RB and disadvantage the FTB in the low-priced region. As the price differential needs to be maintained, the overshooting of price in the high-cost region would have to be mirrored in the low-cost one. The expected inter-regional migration of the marginal buyer from the high-cost region would not occur, suggesting that the high-cost region would not benefit from the pressure release that trading horizontally would provide. Stein's notion of RB 'fishing', setting a high price out of line with current market conditions, corresponds to this increasing price in expectation of future heightened demand.

3.8.2 The Ripple—A Series of Shocks or Persistent Cycle

One could argue that the ripple explanations conform more with the *shock* than the *cycle* perspective. There is no mention of local housing cycles in Meen's explanations, only spillover or diffusion to or from elsewhere, possibly nearby. Wood (2003) suggests it is possible that the South East responds more quickly to national economic shocks or the South East leads the economic cycle and, hence, is a leading region. The national business cycle should leave a mark on national and regional house price activity. This is echoed in Artis and Zhang's (1997) analysis of optimal currency areas. Marchand (1981) finds a dominant Juglar cycle operating in an urban system. This commonality could be a reflection of some non-housing, but pervasive, driving force, such as a national business cycle. Inter-urban demand transmission occurs through trading ties and is reflected in minor, three-month cycles. Dominant Juglar cycles are consistent with Meen's assertion that internal adjustments, not migration, is the most likely explanation of a ripple. A unified market in a cyclic context would be characterised by dominant common periodic elements.

De Groot and Franses' perspective would imply a small number of cycles dominating regional activity. Any asynchronicity would be evident at these key cycles. A cyclical explanation of the ripple effect requires a mechanism to provide common cycles with a delay.

3.9 Consumption

In some fields, there are concepts that emerge both the long and short runs that may present inconsistent views of the world. The simple Keynesian consumption function links consumption expenditure with current disposable income. As Gordon (2013) describes, consumption expenditure and savings are positive functions of income. The marginal propensity to consume and the income multiplier are associated with these functions. The average propensity to consume declines and the savings ratio increases as income rises. An innovation in Keynes's proposition is that those on very low incomes dissave or borrow to maintain a certain level of consumption.

Keynes's model, the absolute income hypothesis, can be seen as a cross-sectional view of consumption, saving and income. This is a snapshot in time. Those that take out a loan today to bolster current consumption will have factored into the decision to borrow to repay that loan (assuming no planned default) tomorrow. There has been an inter-temporal redistribution of consumption. In microeconomics, this intermediation between eras is facilitated by a well-functioning capital market, with the interest rate the cost of impatience in consumption.

3.9.1 Forward-looking Consumption Models

What became known as forward-looking expectations models of income posit that consumers maintain a stable consumption pattern, altering expenditure not with transitory income changes, but when they are viewed as being permanent. Consumption is smoothed relative to income. Two models are commonly discussed: Friedman's permanent income (PIH) and Modigliani's life cycle hypotheses (LCH). Gordon (2013) defines permanent income *as the average annual income that is expected to be received over a period of years in the future*. Consumption is a function of permanent income $C = kY^P$, where C is consumption and Y^P is permanent income. This definition has no clear time horizon over which consumption smoothing takes place. Indeed, the permanent income is subject to revisions. Promotion and/or rise in salary is not automatic, so when it does transpire, a revision of expenditure is not inappropriate.

Transitory income Y^T is positive when income is above trend and negative when below: thus $Y^P = Y - Y^T$. In effect, short-run savings activity absorbs the fluctuations in a business cycle, so that consumption is smoothed and Y^T does not affect income. The accumulation of wealth still follows the long-term profile, but it eliminates the undulations of current circumstances. Consumption can be seen in a similar light with $C = C^T + C^P$. However, transitory consumption becomes problematic. Over the cycle, it sums to zero. The permanent component relates to the amount that consumers plan to consume to maximise their lifetime utility.

Ando and Modigliani's (1963) life-cycle model posits consumption is based on the present value of total resources that the household accrues over a lifetime, suggesting a lifetime budget constraint and that the value of assets directly affect consumption behaviour. People save for their retirement, during which, they may not receive an income but they will consume. This generates a pyramidic shape to total assets.

The profile of income was posited to be flat. However, Fernández-Villaverde and Krueger (2002) reveal the lifetime profile of expenditure, which turns out to be an inverted-U shape. Aggregating up the PIH, Hoover (2012) proposes over the longer run income will reflect the trend in income GDP. In cross-section, the young are making modest contributions to savings, households in the 45–55-age range are saving more heavily, and those over 65 are dissaving. Impatient youngsters, in effect, borrow from earlier generations. In aggregate, borrowings will be a function of the expected growth rate of incomes, interest rates and the stock of wealth.

One implication of the life-cycle model, which is reflected in Hall's (1978) insight on permanent income, is that, with a perfect capital market and perfect foresight, consumption should reflect the lifetime income-constraint from the outset, $C = C^P$. With an uncertain future, cautious consumers build up precautionary savings (Carroll 2001), reducing consumption, possibly despite the ability to borrow from a perfect capital market. The level of caution that some might exhibit would be a function of their environment. In a system where there were no state pension, sickness, or unemployment benefits schemes, precautionary savings would be greater.

Interestingly, Carroll goes on to aver that a credit-constrained environment is much like one with a cautious but impatient consumer. The patient consumer is content to postpone current consumption. With a precautionary saving motive, the impatient consumer *chooses not* to borrow for fear of the consequences of borrowing, whereas the constrained consumer *cannot* borrow against future income to finance current consumption. The outcome is that consumption growth can be strongly tied to predictable income growth, so that permanent income is revised periodically. Caution could drive the consumer to moderate their spending in a recession, leaving consumption expenditure fluctuating in the business cycle range, at odds with a smoothing thesis.

3.9.2 Consumption Constraints and Financial Liberalisation

Expensive durable goods, particularly houses, would be beyond the reach of many consumers without institutional assistance. Means of facilitating the inter-temporal mismatch between accumulating the necessary funds and purchase, such as hire-purchase arrangements and mortgages, are provided by financial institutions. A perfect capital market permits the borrower to borrow against the future value of their income or property. However, the market is replete with information asymmetries leaving the lender with the agency problem in the form of unobserved use of borrowed funds and uncertainty of repayment. To address this, lenders ration funds using metrics, such as loan-to-income.

As recovery of the debt is more likely, lenders differentiate between secured and unsecured lending. With an imperfect market, only some of the present value of their income can be consumed by some beforehand in the form of, say, a mortgage that allows ownership years before the borrower could have accumulated the necessary savings to house purchase.

There is much evidence that the credit channel is a key source of finance for housing, consumption and investment (Muellbauer and Murphy 2008). Aoki et al. (2004) observe that:

1. house prices are strongly cyclical, which leads to substantial variation in households' collateral position over the business cycle;
2. the amount of secured borrowing to finance consumption is closely related to this collateral position;
3. the spread of mortgage rates over the risk-free interest rate varies with the collateral position of each household.

Meen's (2011) highlights a significant shift in credit available from the early 1980s in the UK which was reflected in the US. With credit liberalisation, buyers could borrow more funds for a given level of income (Campbell and Mankiw 1991; Muellbauer 2007). As such, financial markets can be viewed as less imperfect and afford consumers to smooth their consumption better over time. Deregulation of financial services meant easier access to capital for both the buyer and the owner. The owner will borrow more for every level of house price for consumption purposes. The 1980s saw a change in consumption relations. Campbell and Mankiw (1991) argue that a relaxation of a financial constraint allows consumers to behave as the permanent income hypothesis suggests where consumption is a function of permanent income.

Price volatility is conceptualised by focusing on the activity of lenders, asymmetric information and financial multipliers (Aoki et al. 2004; Bernanke and Gertler 1989; Kiyotaki and Moore 1997; Kuang 2014; Palley 2004, 2011; Stein 1995). As the economy picks up, collateral posted to gain approval for secured borrowing rises in value, also borrowers' incomes and net worth improve, resulting in a pro-cyclical credit provision. The greater provision of funds will impact on prices favourably, reinforcing creditworthiness, setting the scene for a financial multiplier effect and the potential for volatile prices. A liberalisation of finance will exaggerate this further, acting as a secular trend, discontinuity or shift in lending metrics. Indeed, Cutler (1995) anticipated that financial deregulation would alter permanently the link between UK household consumption expenditure and housing.

3.9.3 Property, Consumption and the Wealth Effect

If individuals wish to maintain their consumption but buy a house, they would have to borrow more, earn more or save less (Iacoviello and Pavan 2013). Savings and borrowing should offset each over, in either the short or long run. Consumption will reflect long-run income but not short-run income.

Modigliani's model incorporates real assets in the determination of consumption. Property, as a major part of the portfolio of wealth, should be positively linked with consumption. The [present value of] wealth is divided into three elements: labour income in the future; current labour income; and property income. Assets, therefore, play a direct role in determining the level of consumption. A rise in an owner's house price reduces their expected saving, boosting current and future consumption. Ando and Modigliani (1963) suggest that if the increase in house price is viewed as temporary it will not be consolidated with other assets within the perceived stock of wealth.

A positive shock to the economy affects the housing market, boosting prices and the equity of property owners. House prices would have a wealth effect or a collateral effect on consumption (Muellbauer 2007), so that house prices could affect both consumption and the holding of money. Phang (2004) sees the collateral effect funding affecting consumption more directly. Equity withdrawal has allowed the appreciation of house prices to be, in part, extracted by taking out a second mortgage. He also suggests that, if consumers are more optimistic, they are likely to increase their consumption of housing and non-housing goods alike. Furthermore, the purchases of houses are often associated with the acquisition of other complimentary goods, most likely durables.

3.9.4 The Age of the Buyer—Income and Substitution Effects

In his discussion of the PIH, Hoover (2012) points out that the aggregation of the individual to the economy, the age distribution of the populous matters. The young and elderly dissave whilst the middle age are paying off debt or are saving. Muellbauer (2007) posits that there is an aggregate consumption effect due to the down payment an FTB must make. Forced to sacrifice greater current consumption expenditure to find the growing down payment, the first-time buyer is disadvantaged by rising house prices. The down-trader, by contrast, can extract equity to boost their consumption. The first-time buyer sacrifice is posited by Muellbauer to outweigh the last time seller benefit, so, as prices rise consumption may fall.

3.9.5 Consumption of Durable Goods Over the Cycle

It was shown that consumption can be seen in a similar light to income in having permanent and temporary elements, $C = C^T + C^P$. In the absence of uncertainty, there would be no transitory consumption. The permanent component relates to the amount that consumers plan to consume to maximise their lifetime utility. Consumer durable goods are goods that can be consumed over a long period, certainly over a year. In a sense, durables can be seen as investments rather than consumables. They can outlast the quarter or the year and be used many hundreds of times. Indeed, housing is seen as an investment, excluded from household consumption expenditure, but other goods could be excluded also.

Gordon (2013) notes that the purchase of durables can often be postponed during recessions when budgets are tighter, leaving their acquisition for the good times. If so, consumption expenditures on durables would pro-cyclical. As this transitory consumption could be viewed as an investment, it is consistent with the forward-looking consumption models where transitory income adds to wealth.

References

Ali, K., Olfert, M., & Partridge, M. (2011). Urban footprints in rural Canada: Employment spillovers by city size. *Regional Studies, 45*(2), 239–260.

Ando, A., & Modigliani, F. (1963). The 'life-cycle' hypothesis of saving: Aggregate implications and tests. *American Economic Review, 53*(1), 55–84.

Aoki, K., Proudmand, J., & Vlieghe, G. (2004). House prices, consumption and monetary policy: A financial accelerator approach. *Journal of Financial Intermediation, 13,* 414–435.

Armstrong, H., & Taylor, J. (2000). *Regional economics and policy*. London: Harvester Wheatsheaf.

Artis, M. (2006). What do we know about currency unions. *Bank of England Quarterly Bulletin,* (Summer), 243–255.

Artis, M., & Zhang, W. (1997). International business cycles and the ERM: Is there a European business cycle? *International Journal of Finance and Economics, 2,* 1–16.

Artis, M., Chouliarakis, G., & Harischandra, P. (2011). Business cycle synchronisation since 1880. *Manchester School, 79*(2), 173–207.

Benito, A. (2006, March). *How does the down-payment constraint affect the UK housing market* (Bank of England Working Paper 294).

Bennett, R., Hanning, R., & Wilson, A. (1985). Spatial structure, spatial interaction, and their integration: A review of alternative models. *Environment and Planning A, 17,* 625–645.

Bernanke, B., & Gertler, M. (1989). Agency costs, net worth, and business fluctuations. *American Economic Review, 79*(1), 14–31.

Bogart, W. (1998). *The economics of cities and suburbs.* Upper Saddle River, NJ: Prentice Hall.

Borgatti, S., & Everett, M. (1999). Models of core/periphery structures. *Social Networks, 21*(4), 375–395.

Brown, G. (1984). Real estate cycles alter the valuation perspective. *Appraisal Journal, 5*(4), 539–549.

Brühl, M., & Lizieri, C. (1994). Centralism vs. federalism: Implications for regional diversification. *Journal of Property Valuation and Investment, 12*(1), 59–73.

Burns, L. (1987). Regional economic integration and national economic growth. *Regional Studies, 21,* 327–339.

Campbell, J., & Mankiw, N. G. (1991). The response of consumption to income: A cross-country investigation. *European Economic Review, 35*(4), 723–756.

Carroll, C. (2001). A theory of the consumption function, with and without liquidity constraints. *Journal of Economic Perspectives, 15*(3), 23–45.

Clayton, J. (1998). Further evidence on real estate market efficiency. *The Journal of Real Estate Research, 15*(1/2), 41–57.

Cutler, J. (1995). The housing market and the economy. *Bank of England Quarterly Bulletin,* August, 260–269.

De Goei, B., Burger, M., Van Oort, F., & Kitson, M. (2010). Functional polycentrism and urban network development in the Greater South East, United Kingdom: Evidence from commuting patterns, 1981–2001. *Regional Studies, 44*(9), 1149–1170.

De Grauwe, P. (2003). *The economics of monetary integration* (5th ed.). Oxford: OUP.

De Groot, B., & Franses, P. (2008). Stability though cycles. *Technological Forecasting and Social Change, 75,* 301–311.

Derudder, B., Taylor, P., Witlox, F., & Catalano, G. (2003). Hierarchical tendencies and regional patterns in the world city network: A global urban analysis of 234 cities. *Regional Studies, 37*(9), 875–886.

Dicks, M. (1989). The housing market. *Bank of England Quarterly Bulletin,* February, 66–75.

DiPasquale, D., & Wheaton, W. (1996). *Urban economics and real estate markets.* Englewood Cliffs, NJ: Prentice Hall.

Duranton, G., & Puga, D. (2005). From sectoral to functional urban specialization. *Journal of Urban Economics, 57*(2), 343–370.

Dusansky, R., & Wilson, R. (1993). The demand for housing: Theoretical considerations. *Journal of Economic Theory, 61,* 120–138.

Fatas, A. (1997). Countries or regions? Lessons from the EMS experience. *European Economic Review, 41,* 743–751.

Fernández-Villaverde, J., & Krueger, D. (2002). *Consumption over the life cycle: Some facts from the consumer expenditure survey data* (NBER Working Paper 9382). http://www.nber.org/papers/w9382. Accessed 1 Dec 2014.

Fernandez, R., Hofman, A., & Albers, M. (2016). London and New York as a safe deposit box for the transnational wealth elite. *Environment and Planning A, 48*(12), 2443–2461.

Friedmann, J. (1973). *Urbanisation, planning and national development.* Beverly Hills: Sage.

Godfrey, B., & Zhou, Y. (1999). Ranking world cities: Multinational corporation and the global urban hierarchy. *Urban Geography, 20*(3), 268–281.

Gordon, R. (2013). *Macroeconomics* (12th ed.). Prentice Hall: New York.

Grover, R., & Grover, C. (2014). Property bubbles—A transitory phenomenon. *Journal of Property Investment and Finance, 32*(2), 208–222.

Hall, R. (1978). Stochastic implications of the life cycle-permanent income hypothesis: Theory and evidence. *Journal of Political Economy, 86*(6), 971–987.

Harrison, F. (2005). *Boom bust: House prices, banking and the depression of 2010*. London: Shepheard-Walwyn.

Herbert, D., & Thomas, C. (1995). *Cities in space: City as place* (2nd ed.). David Fulton: London.

Higgins, B. (1983). From growth poles to systems of interaction in space. *Growth and Change, 14*(4), 3–13.

Hirschman, A. (1958). *The strategies of economic development*. New Haven: Yale University Press.

Holly, S., Pesaran, H., & Yamagata, T. (2011). The spatio-temporal diffusion of house prices in the UK. *Journal of Urban Economics, 69*(1), 2–23.

Hoover, K. (2012). *Applied intermediate macroeconomics*. New York, NY: CUP.

Iacoviello, M., & Pavan, M. (2013). Housing and debt over the life cycle and over the business cycle. *Journal of Monetary Economics, 60*, 221–238.

Jones, C., & Leishman, C. (2006). Spatial dynamics of the housing market: An interurban perspective. *Urban Studies, 43*(7), 1041–1059.

Jordà, Ò., Schularick, M., & Taylor, M. (2016). The great mortgaging: Housing finance, crises and business cycles. *Economic Policy, 31*(85), 107–152.

Kiyotaki, N., & Moore, J. (1997). Credit cycles. *Journal of Political Economy, 105*(2), 211–248.

Krugman, P. (1991). *Geography and trade*. Cambridge, MA: MIT Press.

Kuang, P. (2014). A model of housing and credit cycles with imperfect market knowledge. *European Economic Review, 70*, 419–437.

Leamer, E. (2007). *Housing is the business cycle* (Working Paper 13428, NBER).

Leamer, E. (2015). Housing is the business cycle: What survives the lessons of 2008–09? *Journal of Money Credit and Banking, 47*(1), 43–50.

Limtanakool, N., Dijst, M., & Schwanen, T. (2007). A theoretical framework and methodology for characterising national urban systems on the basis of flows of people: Empirical evidence for France and Germany. *Urban Studies, 44*(11), 2123–2145.

Limtanakool, N., Schwanen, T., & Dijst, M. (2009). Developments in the Dutch urban system on the basis of flows. *Regional Studies, 43*(2), 179–196.

Madsen, J. (2012). A behavioural model of house prices. *Journal of Economics Behaviour & Organisation, 82,* 21–38.

Marchand, C. (1981). Maximum entropy spectra and the spatial and temporal dimensions of economic fluctuations in an urban system. *Geographical Analysis, 13,* 95–116.

McCann, P. (2001). *Urban and regional economics.* Oxford: Oxford University Press.

McCombie, J. (1988). A synoptic view of regional growth and unemployment: II—The Post-Keynesian theory. *Urban Studies, 25,* 399–417.

McDonald, J. (1985). Expectations and urban housing prices. *Urban Studies, 22,* 543–549.

Meen, G. (1999). Regional house prices and the ripple effect: A new interpretation. *Housing Studies, 14*(6), 733–753.

Meen, G. (2011). The economic consequences of mortgage debt. *Journal of Housing and the Build Environment, 26*(3), 263–276.

Montagnoli, A., & Nagayasu, J. (2015). UK house price convergence clubs and spillovers. *Journal of Housing Economics, 30,* 50–58.

Morrow-Jones, H., & Wenning, M. (2005). The housing ladder, the housing life-cycle and the housing life-course: Upward and downward movement among repeat home-buyers in a US metropolitan housing market. *Urban Studies, 42*(10), 1739–1754.

Muellbauer, J. (2007). Housing, credit and consumer expenditure. In *Proceedings-Economic Policy Symposium-Jackson Hole* (pp. 267–334). Kansas City: Federal Reserve Bank of Kansas City.

Muellbauer, J., & Murphy, A. (2008). Housing markets and the economy: The assessment. *Oxford Review Economic Policy, 24*(1), 1–33.

Mundell, R. (1961). A theory of optimal currency areas. *American Economic Review, 51,* 657–664.

Myrdal, G. (1957). *Economic theory and underdeveloped regions.* London: Duckworth.

Olfert, M., & Stabler, J. (1999). Multipliers in a central place hierarchy. *Growth and Change, 30,* 299–302.

Palley, T. (2004). Debt, aggregate demand, and the business cycle: An analysis in the spirit of Kaldor and Minsky. *Journal of Post-Keynesian Economics, 16*(3), 371–389.

Palley, T. (2010). The limits of Minsky's financial instability hypothesis as an explanation of the crisis. *Monthly Review, 61*(11), 28–43.

Palley, T. (2011). A theory of Minsky super-cycles and financial crises. *Contributions to Political Economy, 30*(1), 31–46.

Partridge, M., Rickman, D., Ali, K., & Olfert, M. (2009). Do new economic geography agglomeration shadows underlie current population dynamics across the urban hierarchy? *Papers in Regional Science, 88*(2), 445–466.

Perroux, F. (1950). Economic space, theory and applications. *Quarterly Journal of Economics, 64,* 89–104.

Persaud, A. (2016). *Breaking the link between housing cycles, banking crises, and recession.* City Political Economy Research Centre. https://www.city.ac.uk/__data/assets/pdf_file/0019/312571/CITYPERC-WPS-201602.pdf. Accessed 2 Jan 2017.

Phang, S. (2004). House prices and aggregate consumption: Do they move together? Evidence from Singapore. *Journal of Housing Economics, 13*(2), 101–119.

Pred, A. (1966). *The spatial dynamics of urban growth in the United States, 1800–1914.* Cambridge, MA: MIT Press.

Pred, A. (1980). *Urban growth and city systems in the United States, 1840–1860.* Cambridge, MA: Harvard University Press.

Pritchett, C. (1984). Forecasting the impact of real estate cycles on investment. *Real Estate Review, 13*(4), 85–89.

Pyhrr, S., Roulac, S., & Born, W. (1999). Real estate cycles and their strategic implications for investors and portfolio managers in the global economy. *The Journal of Real Estate Research, 18*(1), 7–68.

Richardson, H. (1978). *Regional and urban economics.* Middlesex: Penguin.

Scanlon, K., & Whitehead, C. (2011). The UK mortgage market: Responding to volatility. *Journal of Housing and the Build Environment, 26,* 277–293.

Scott, A. (1998). *Regions and the world economy.* Oxford: Oxford University Press.

Smith, L., & Ho, M. (1996). The relative price differential between higher and lower priced homes. *Journal of Housing Economics, 5,* 1–17.

Smith, B., & Tesarek, W. (1991). House prices and regional real estate cycles: Market adjustments in Houston. *Real Estate Economics, 19*(3), 396–416.

Sommervoll, D., Borgersen, T.-A., & Wennemo, T. (2010). Endogenous housing market cycles. *Journal of Banking & Finance, 34*(3), 557–567.

Spotton, B. (1997). Financial instability reconsidered: Orthodox theories verses historical facts. *Journal of Economic Literature, 31,* 175–195.

Stein, J. (1995). Prices and trading volume in the housing market: A model with downpayment effects. *The Quarterly Journal of Economics, 110*, 379–405.

Storper, M. (1995). The resurgence of regional economies, ten years later: The region as a Nexus of untraded interdependencies. *European Urban and Regional Studies, 2*, 191–222.

Storper, M. (1997). *The regional world*. London: Guilford Press.

Storper, M., & Walker, R. (1989). *The capitalist imperative. Territory, technology, and industrial growth*. Blackwell: Oxford.

Terluin, I. (2003). Differences in economic development in rural regions of advanced countries: An overview and critical analysis of theories. *Journal of Rural Studies, 19*, 327–344.

Van Duijn, J. J. (1983). *The long wave in economic life*. London: Allen & Unwin.

Wood, R. (2003). The information of regional house prices: Can they be used to improve national house price forecasts? *Bank of England Quarterly Bulletin, 43*(3), 304–314.

4

Spectral Analysis and Other Pairwise Techniques

Abstract The examination of data entails spectral analysis, a time series approach in the frequency domain. The issue of de-trending data is discussed in terms of high-pass filtering. Spectral analysis will be discussed. This includes an exposition of the power spectrum, phase, and coherence. Innovations in the areas of adjusted gain, cohesion, and synchronicity are also outlined. The latter is a new measure that complements cohesion. Long-run relations are assessed using unit root tests. These are discussed in terms of recent innovations in pairwise econometric work due to Pesaran.

Keywords Power spectrum · De-trending data · Spectral analysis
Granger-causality

4.1 Introduction

The examination of data entails, in the main, spectral analysis: a time series approach in the frequency domain. This approach offers an unusual perspective, where hidden periodicities are revealed possibly highlighting

D. Gray, *Cycles in the UK Housing Economy*,
DOI 10.1007/978-3-319-63348-0_4

unexpected relationships. It requires long series of unbroken data, and analysis is on a pairwise basis, so does come with limitations. The issue of detrending data is discussed in terms of high-pass filtering. Spectral analysis will be discussed. This includes an exposition of the power spectrum, phase, and coherence. Innovations in the areas of adjusted gain, cohesion, and synchronicity are also outlined. The latter is a new measure that complements cohesion. Long-run relations are assessed using unit root tests. These are discussed in terms of recent innovations due to Pesaran (2007a, b).

4.2 Filters and Cycles

A time series X_t can be seen as comprising a growth or trend element g_t and a cyclical element x_t such that $X_t = g_t + x_t$. Hodrick-Prescott filter (H-P) smooths out x_t so as to remove seasonal components. The process entails minimising

$$\sum_{t=1}^{T} x_t^2 + \lambda \sum_{t=1}^{T} \left[(g_t - g_{t-1}) - (g_{t-1} - g_{t-2})\right]^2$$

where λ is a positive number that penalises variability in the trend component. The greater the λ is set, the more smooth the series. H-P filter acts to remove a trend from the data by solving a least square problem. For quarterly data, λ is commonly set to 1600.

The filter is not without its critics. Guay and St-Amant (2005) and Cogley and Nason (1995) find that the Hodrick-Prescott filters can inject distortions in the filtered series. Cogley and Nason, find that, in data that is difference stationary, amplitude is greater at business cycles frequencies but damped at short and longer frequencies. Guay and St-Amant (2005) find that the H-P adequately characterises the series dynamics when the peak of the power spectrum is at business cycle frequencies. If the low frequencies dominate the spectrum, the H-P is poor at extracting the cyclical component. Constructing Swedish real estate indices, whilst noting the criticisms of Guay and St-Amant (2005), Witkiewicz (2002) uses the H-P filter. He reviews the literature that mounts a robust defence of the filter. He concludes that the identification of cycles and turning points are vital for the institutional investor. Canova (1999) finds that the H-P filter is a useful method for detrending compared with differencing. Authors have used the filter to extract business cycle effects from time series. King and Rebelo (1993) show that the H-P filter can render any integrated process of up to the fourth order stationary. Pakko (2000) finds that the algorithm acts like a high-pass filter and is superior to differencing for spectral work.

Phillips and Jin (2015) find the order of magnitude of λ in the H-P filter in relation to the sample size turns out to be of great importance. They suggest that the H-P filter does not typically eliminate a time series' unit root, explaining the Cogley and Nasan (1995) spurious cycle findings. Rather, the smoothing parameter should increase with sample size. They show that filters have the capacity to capture most of these different forms of trend. If used with care and with priors that reject economic thinking about the underlying processes at work in determining latent variables, they may be successfully employed in empirical work to estimate such latent variables in the observed data. Also, reviewing the parameter choice, Harvey and Trimbur (2008) conclude that for quarterly US GDP, 1600 is a good option. However, the investment cycle is better extracted with a filter setting of 32,000.

Igan et al. (2011) point out that differencing acts as a high-band filter. It has a disadvantage that the square gain functions deviate substantially from that of an ideal high-band filter. The widespread use of differencing is, therefore, 'surprising'.

As a key theme concerns cyclicality, alternative filters are utilised. Butterworth's (BW) and Christiano-Fitzgerald's (CF) filters are employed. The settings for the CF are minimum and maximum periodicities of 2 and 40. The BW is set with a maximum value of 40 and MA(2).

4.3 Cross-Spectral Analysis

The theoretical spectrum divides up time series data into a set of components that are orthogonal such that the spectrum reveals the relative power at each frequency corresponding to the variance at each periodicity assessed.

4.3.1 Covariance Stationary Time Series

The shape of the spectrum highlights the variance associated with each frequency. Sharp peaks denote a high concentration. The autocovariance $\gamma_{XX}(k) = E\left[(X_{t+k} - \mu)(X_t - \mu)\right]$ in the time domain is represented as the population spectrum, $s_{XX}(\omega) = \frac{1}{2\pi}\sum_{k=-\infty}^{\infty}\gamma_{XX}(k)e^{-ik\omega}$, in the frequency domain. As it is symmetrical around $\omega = 0$, this is transformed into $s_{XX}(\omega) = \frac{1}{2\pi}\left[\gamma_0 + 2\sum_{k=1}^{\infty}\gamma_{XX}(k)\cos(\omega k)\right]$. The sample periodogram, $\hat{s}_{XX}(\omega) = \frac{1}{2\pi}\left[\hat{\gamma}_0 + 2\sum_{k=1}^{T-1}\hat{\gamma}_{XX}(k)\cos(\omega k)\right]$, can be explored for autocovariance at various frequencies. The sample periodogram is not a consistent estimator of the theoretical spectrum: the periodogram is not well behaved as the number of frequencies is a function of T but variance is not. As such, the periodogram is smoothed using a Parzen approach.

One question to address is whether coefficients indicate white noise. Hughes-Hallett and Richter (2004), Levy and Dezhbakhsh (2003), in combination, proffer two alternative methods to address this. One could consider whether the values of the spectrum fall outside the confidence interval for the bound of the density value at zero frequency. Alternatively, one could examine whether the lower (upper) band of the confidence interval density values are above (below) the upper (lower) bound of the density value at zero frequency. The latter is a more onerous test to pass.

Bivariate analysis entails cross-spectral analysis. The equivalent of covariance and correlation in the time domain are cospectrum and coherence. The cospectrum between X and Y at frequency ω_j represents the covariance between X and Y at frequency ω_j. The cross-spectrum is given by $s_{XY}(\omega) = \frac{1}{2\pi}\sum_{k=-\infty}^{\infty}\gamma_{XY}(k)(\cos(\omega k) - i\sin(\omega k))$. This can be broken down in the real and imaginary parts $s_{XY}(\omega) = c_{XY}(\omega) + iq_{XY}(\omega)$, the cospectrum $c_{XY}(\omega) = \frac{1}{2\pi}\sum_{k=-\infty}^{\infty}\gamma_{XY}(k)\cos(\omega k)$, and the quadrature $-q_{XY}(\omega) = \frac{1}{2\pi}\sum_{k=-\infty}^{\infty}\gamma_{XY}(k)\sin(\omega k)$. The quadrature spectrum $q_{XY}(\omega_j)$ is the imaginary part of the cross-spectrum. It reveals out-of-phase covariance between X and Y at frequency ω_j. X and Y may both have a high proportion of their variance at frequency ω_j but low covariance, as the components are out of phase.

Of key importance to cross-spectral analysis is coherence, the equivalent of correlation. If the coherence is large, it indicates the degree to which X and Y are jointly influenced at a common frequency ω_j. The theoretical squared coherence is given by $C_{XY}{}^2(\omega) = \frac{|s_{XY}(\omega)|^2}{s_X(\omega)s_Y(\omega)}$.

An approach due to Smith (2001) and reviewed by Wang (2003) entails a cross-spectral analysis of the impact of the 1987 crash on equity markets of the Pacific Rim. Using coherence among pairs of asset markets for portfolio construction purposes, Smith reveals intensification through increased coherence. Cross-spectra are estimated over a set of frequencies, not just one, so finding heightened coherence at one frequency may conflict with evidence at another. He uses Wilcoxon's Z-statistic to assess whether the two spectra of coherence are drawn from the same population. This corresponds to a null of no change against an alternative of weaker or stronger links.

A recent innovation due to Croux et al. (2001) is the notion of cohesion. This takes the real portion of the cross-spectrum and is given by $coh_{XY}(\omega) = \frac{c_{XY}(\omega)}{\sqrt{s_{XX}(\omega)s_{YY}(\omega)}}$. This ranges between –1 and +1. Their interpretation is akin to correlation. By implication, the quadrature spectrum, the out-of-phase covariance between X and Y could also be adapted. Describing it as a measure of synchronisation is defined as $syn_{XY}(\omega) = \frac{q_{XY}(\omega)}{\sqrt{s_{XX}(\omega)s_{YY}(\omega)}}$. This ranges between -1 and +1. So that the correlation in the frequency domain can be subdivided into *in-* and *out-*of-phase portions. In practice, where the two variables are closely associated, it has a similar frequency profile to phase.

A further use for this division is related to coherence. Coherence [squared] can be subdivided into $C_{XY}^2(\omega) = coh_{XY}^2(\omega) + syn_{XY}^2(\omega)$. As such, squared coherence is subdivided into the portion in phase and the portion out of phase. If in phase, cohesion and coherence provide the same information. X and Y could have a high coherence and a low cohesion. This is consistent with a pair of regional indices with similar price dynamics but out of phase by ¼ω_j. Phase, Wilson and Okunev (1999) argue, is an important measure. If the two financial series are out of phase by ½ω_j, the phase value is dislocated by a factor of π radians or 180° degrees. The assets are orthogonal or perfect complements to have in a portfolio. When discussing portfolio diversification strategies, they calculate phase value's time domain equivalent at the peak of cospectra between real estate and stock markets, i.e. at a point in the phase diagram.

The Gain is given by $G_{XY}(\omega) = \frac{|s_{XY}(\omega)|}{s_{XX}(\omega)}$. Gain is the equivalent of a regression coefficient in the time domain but at given frequencies. That is, gain explains how amplitude of one variable is translated into the amplitude of the other (Sun et al. 2007). A small gain value at frequency ω indicates that the first variable has little influence on the second. With a phase shift, the gain can be interpreted as the regression coefficient in the time domain as if the series was lagged sufficiently to eliminate that phase shift (Levy 1994).

The phase value gives a notion of leading (if positive) of the first series X over the second Y at frequency ω_j. The phase angle $P_{XY}(\omega) = \tan^{-1} \frac{-q_{XY}(\omega)}{c_{XY}(\omega)}$ is converted into a time shift tau τ by phase angle/angular frequency $P_{XY}(\omega_j)/\omega_j$ which can be written as $P_{XY}(\omega_j)/2\pi f_j$ (Harvey 1993).

To translate Meen's ripple definition into the frequency domain, it implies that all regions can modelled by sinusoidal series that are subject to a phase shift or delay relative to the reference cycle. The polycentric urban, or the balanced, models would be characterised by lower coherence and peaks in the power spectrum that are weakly reflected in the reference series' profile, indicative of local cycles, and distinctive industrial bases (Marchand 1981).

Each region should lead or lag the reference cycle, related to the distance from London. The national series would have a relatively strong coherence with regions in the middle part of England. The imaginary element inherent in coherence which accommodates the asynchronicity means that the coherence value at ω_j is unaffected by the asynchronicity. However, squared cohesion declines with an increasing asynchronicity. This implies that a ripple at a common cycle is characterised by region–nation relation where the coherence is high and stable but there is an inverse relationship between squared synchronicity and squared cohesion.

From a systems view, London should be attuned to the UK housing reference series, influencing it more than any other housing market. London and the southern regions should lead East Anglia, as part of its commuting shed. Regions where the second-tier cities are based, such as Birmingham or Leeds, should have relatively high power and coherence suggesting the West Midlands and Yorkshire-Humberside should be attuned to the reference series. However, the second-tier nodes should be 'attuned' to the national cycle, but not necessarily as highly as the dominant one. Higher-tier nodes of a hierarchical system with growth pole characteristics should exhibit greater growth, which should feed through to house prices. A low-order node could be characterised by a modest effect on, or response to, the reference series, suggesting gain would be modest.

The pairwise analysis entails house price variations in the region, HP_r, represented as a function of national price variations HP_N: $HP_r(\omega) = H_{r1}(\omega)\ HP_N(\omega)$, where $H_{r1}(\omega)$ is a transfer function from the nation to the region (Marchand 1981; Rosenthal 1986; Tiller and Bednarzik 1983). The frequency response function $H(\omega)$ is complex function comprising both gain and phase, as given by $H(\omega) = G(\omega)e^{i\varphi(\omega)}$ (see Chatfield 1989, Section 9.32). As such, the two expressions can be seen as

$$HP_r(\omega) = G_{r1}(\omega)e^{i\varphi_{r1}(\omega)}HP_N(\omega) \tag{4.1}$$

$$HP_N(\omega) = G_{r2}(\omega)e^{i\varphi_{r2}(\omega)}HP_r(\omega) \tag{4.2}$$

Gain 1 for region r, $G_{r1}(\omega_j)$, identifies how the amplitude of the house price cycles in $HPN(\omega)$ is translated into the amplitude of $HP_r(\omega)$ at frequency ω_j. The range of frequencies captures the division between longer and shorter cyclical elements. Assuming the two series were measured in the same units, Gain 1 will tend to exceed unity when the regional amplitude is greater than that of the reference series' value; it is amplified (Dunn 1983). Gain 2, $G_{r2}(\omega)$, involves the reverse. To place them in common units, the gain values are adjusted by the standard deviation of both filtered series, which generates the equivalent of a beta value in regression. The adjusted Gain 1 value is interpreted as the impact of a change of one standard deviation in $\mathrm{HP}_N(\omega)$ is translated into the amplitude of $\mathrm{HP}_r(\omega)$ assessed in standard deviations of the latter.

Wilson and Okunev (1999), Sun et al. (2007) and Liow (2007) use $\phi_{r1}(\omega)$ values converted into the time domain (as tau values) to reveal leads and lags between real estate price indices. Spectral analysis is useful in that a pair of regions have different leads against a reference cycle, that differential is the same as one region has over the other. So, using a reference series is an efficient means of revealing a ripple effect.

As the national series for both FTB and RB are available, it is possible to compare region with the corresponding national reference cycle. Thus, the configuration found in Gray (2013) could be subdivided into two:-

$$HP_{rFTB}(\omega) = G_{rFTB}(\omega)e^{i\varphi_{rFTB}(\omega)}HP_{FTB}(\omega) \tag{4.3}$$

$$HP_{rRB}(\omega) = G_{rRB}(\omega)e^{i\varphi_{rRB}(\omega)}HP_{RB}(\omega) \tag{4.4}$$

so that comparisons can be made.

As Benito (2006) tests and OMR predicts, RB price volatility should be greater than FTB. Sommervoll et al. (2010) suggest that flat and house will be subject to periodic dramatic falls in prices with the downturn in flat prices leading to an amplified collapse in houses. Stein suggests there could also be enhanced volatility in pricing if the trades are between existing owners. Greater volatility should also be evident in the gain values. The RB prices should be more volatile with a value greater than one for gain from FTB to RB.

Sommervoll et al. suggest that flat and house prices would have a common cycle. This would be reflected in high coherence values at key frequencies. Stein modelled interaction among RB-enhanced volatility in pricing if the trades are between existing owners. Gray (2015) finds more than one frequency in dwelling prices, possibly suggesting FTB might drive one and RB the another.

Mayer (1993), Smith and Tesarek (1991) anticipate higher volatility for more expensive housing. By implication, London should have the highest level of volatility, particularly in RB housing, so that the gain value should be the largest in the system for both FTB and RB with the latter larger than the former. However, from a regional-ripple perspective, so long as the regions contain significant populations that can commute to the highest cost region, these lower price regions will have greater volatility than the highest priced regions. Indeed, this will particularly affect the FTB. The greater volatility inherent in high-cost housing is absorbed by those out-priced locally looking elsewhere.

4.4 Finance, Income, and Consumption

Levy and Dezhbakhsh (2003) find the UK has a peak of the power spectrum for real GDP at around 6–8 year cycles. Following Leamer, one would expect that the business cycles would interact with the house price cycles, so the power spectrum of the reference GDP and housing series should show this. Consumption, posited to be smoothed, will have a lower variance in high frequencies but common variance at low. Consistent with the PIH, it should have a lower variance at the business cycle than GDP's.

One would anticipate finance for house purchase should reflect the cost of house purchase. Secured lending, predominantly for house purchase should have the same sort of profile as house prices. By contrast, unsecured lending should reflect consumption smoothing. Following the PIH, in a recession, consumers borrow to smooth. As such this should be counter-cyclical. However, lending is posited to be constrained by agency problems and rationed by lending metrics. As such, changes in household income would affect creditworthiness. Unsecured and secured lending could be pro-cyclical.

4.5 Granger Causality

A concept of causality commonly adopted in the econometric sense is Granger-causality. Granger (1969), makes two key assumptions that underlay the causality test. First, the future cannot cause the past and second, that 'a cause' contains unique information about 'an effect' that is not available elsewhere. As Hamilton (1994) notes, although the discussion of Granger causality concerns forecasting, the econometric test normally involves only current and past observed data. To identify Granger causality and/or feedback both (4.5) and (4.6) are estimated, and joint tests of significance are conducted on the coefficients. If $\phi_{2j} \neq 0$ in (4.5), x_2 Granger-causes x_1. If $\phi_{3j} \neq 0$ in (4.6), x_1 Granger-causes x_2. If both $\phi_{2j} \neq 0$ in (4.5) and $\phi_{3j} \neq 0$ in (4.6), there is Granger causality in both directions (feedback). Thus, the Granger causality test can be used to identify unidirectional causation and feedback.

$$x_{1t} = \alpha_1 + \sum_{j=1}^{p} \phi_{1j} x_{1t-j} + \sum_{j=1}^{p} \phi_{2j} x_{2t-j} + e_{1t} \tag{4.5}$$

$$x_{2t} = \alpha_2 + \sum_{j=1}^{p} \phi_{3j} x_{1t-j} + \sum_{j=1}^{p} \phi_{4j} x_{2t-j} + e_{2t} \tag{4.6}$$

As lagged dependent variables are involved, the F test for Granger causality is only valid asymptotically. The F test and the χ^2 or Wald test are asymptotically equivalent (Hamilton 1994: p. 305).

With p lags of x_{1t} and x_{2t} in (4.5), $k = 2p$ and $q = p$. The null hypothesis that x_2 does not Granger-cause x_1 is rejected if the resulting F value is greater than a critical value, $F(q, T\text{–}k\text{–}1)$, at say the 5% level, or if the resulting value χ^2 is greater than a critical value for $\chi^2(q)$. Then, one concludes that x_2 causes x_1 in the Granger sense (Hamilton 1994). Lütkepohl (1982) discusses the problem of inference in Granger causality tests when variables are omitted from the information set, arguing that a limited set could lead to spurious conclusions of Granger causality when it does not exist, or failing to identify Granger causality when it does exist. Granger (1988) argues that if the forecast of a time series variable x_{1t} conditional on a set of information with x_{2t} is no better than the forecast of x_{1t} conditional on a set of information without x_{2t}, then x_{2t} does not cause x_{1t} in the Granger sense. The pairwise approach has the most limited set of information.

4.6 Unit Roots

Standard unit root tests are applied to the regional house price and other variables and to the differential with the UK in levels. The tests are the Augmented Dickey Fuller test (ADF), plus alternatives due to Park and Fuller (1995) (ADF_pf) and Kwiatkowski et al. (1992) (KPSS). The standard unit root ADF test procedure involves the expression:

$$\Delta x_{it} = \alpha_{i0} + (\rho_i - 1)x_{it-1} + \beta_i t + \sum_{j=1}^{p} \alpha_{ij}\Delta x_{it-j} + e_{it}. \quad (4.7)$$

Pesaran (2007a, b) shows that with panels, where there is cross-sectional dependence, the Im-Pesaran-Shin (IPS) unit root test suffers from size distortions. To address this, he proposes the Cross-sectional Augmented IPS (CIPS), a modification of the ADF. There are four stages to generating the CIPS statistic. To establish cross-sectional interdependence across the N-variables, Pesaran uses a CD statistic, generated from the residuals e_{it} in (4.7).

$$CD = \sqrt{\frac{2T}{N(N-1)}}\left(\sum_{i=1}^{N-1}\sum_{j=i+1}^{N}\hat{\rho}_{ij}\right) \sim N(0,1) \quad \hat{\rho}_{ij} = \frac{\sum_{t=1}^{T}\hat{e}_{it}\hat{e}_{jt}}{\sqrt{\left(\sum_{t=1}^{T}\hat{e}_{it}^{2}\right)\left(\sum_{t=1}^{T}\hat{e}_{jt}^{2}\right)}}$$

If the residuals are interdependent, Pesaran recommends the generation of the cross-sectional ADF (CADF). The CADF procedure involves the expression,

$$\Delta x_{it} = \alpha_{i0} + (\rho_i - 1)x_{it-1} + \beta_i t + \sum_{j=1}^{p} \alpha_{ij}\Delta x_{it-j} + (\theta - 1)\bar{x}_{t-1} + \sum_{j=1}^{p} \delta_j \Delta \bar{x}_{t-j} + e_{it}, \quad (4.8)$$

where

p is the order of the lag polynomial
$e_{it} \sim \text{iid}(0, \sigma_{ie}^2)$
t is a time trend
$\bar{x}_{t-1}$ is the mean of all the values of x at time, $t - 1$.

The fourth stage involves the CIPS statistic, which is defined as $N^{-1} \sum_{i=1}^{N} ADF_i$, where ADF_i is the ADF statistic on the coefficient $(\rho_i - 1)$ in (4.8). The CIPS, like the IPS test, has a null of unit root.

4.7 Application of Unit Root Tests and Granger Causality

Meen (1999) asserted that the regional to national house price ratio should exhibit little or no long-term trend. Holmes (2007) and Holmes and Grimes (2008) use region-nation differentials to establish convergence. The latter's focus is principal components analysis and the use of panel unit root tests. Assume that there are two distinct housing markets in the UK, following distinct paths or trends. The UK house price series, which is a weighted average of the regional ones, will display a path somewhere in between. As the UK index is not following either common trend, it is not clear that it would exhibit cointegration with any one region. Carvalho and Harvey (2005) argue that a unified market exists in this Holmes and Grimes (2008) region-nation approach when all regions are converging to the national average. If one is diverging, this will affect the reference national average. In regional system models, such as cumulative causation or urban systems theory, dominant nodes drive activity in the periphery. One might expect price dispersion to reflect a hierarchy and ripple effect explanations to incorporate such perspectives.

As adopted by Abbott and De Vita (2013), Pesaran (2007a) can be applied to each regional pair. A variant of pairwise cointegration is to test for stationarity using $x_{rt} = \ln HP_{rt} - \ln HP_{Nt}$ in (4.7). Non-stationarity in differential implies non-cointegration.

4.8 Cycle Perspective in the Time Domain

A *cycle* perspective in can be conceptualised in terms of business cycles with a simple Mundell (1961) type model in the time domain. Assume a nation contains two regions, each specialising in one industry. Each industry is characterised by a distinct single sinusoidal series, which is the equivalent of a dominant regional cycle. The cycle orthogonality ensures a complete absence of a measure of co-movement. As such, portfolio theory suggests the nation having a lower variance than the regions. The distinct regional structures result in a reduction of one half. Of course, specialisation comes with interregional trade. As such, one region's income cycle will affect the others, leading to an increase in regional and national correlations.

A single common sinusoidal periodicity with synchronisation implies the national and regional cycles will correlate with a value of one. Thus, as implied by Artis, trade should lead to similar regional cycles possibly in a manner suggested by Marchand (1981). Intra-industry trade would imply a common cycle for both regions.

Housing, reflecting local conditions, should follow the above. Indeed, cross-border commuting or migration is analogous to trade in linking regional cycles. With cross-border commuting in a multi-regional setting, regions should be in close proximity. Trade and migration are spatially non-specific. They would make all regional cycle more similar.

A ripple is posited to reflect asynchronicity at cycle ω_j. With the nation acting as a central benchmark, the lagging region subject to a phase shift of D can be modelled by $\cos(\omega_j + D)$. Correspondingly, the leading region can be expressed as $\cos(\omega_j - D)$. Using $\cos(\omega_j \pm D) = \cos\omega_j \times \cos D \mp \sin\omega_j \times \sin D$, the national reference series can be expressed as $\cos\omega_j \times \cos D$. In other words, the nation will have the same cycle as the regions but the amplitude of the nation's cycle will be cos $D \times$ either region's. The correlation of the regional cycles with the nation's will again be cos D. By implication, the correlation of the two regional series will be cos($2D$).

One implication for portfolio analysis is that extent of the asynchronicity, D, relative to the cycle periodicity, ω, affects the correlation. If $D > \frac{1}{4}\omega_j$, the national series is negatively correlated with the regions suggesting a favourable outcome for spreading risk. Indeed, if $2D = \frac{1}{4}\omega_j$, the correlation of the two regional cycles is zero, and each is correlated with the nation with a value of $\sqrt{0.5}$. If $D = \frac{1}{4}\omega_j$, the amplitude of the portfolio [national series] is zero. In other words, the effect of asynchronicity can be just as useful as a distinct industrial mix: lower cycle correlations and a smaller portfolio variance (Wilson and Okunev 1999).

The above implies that a ripple in a cycle perspective requires common regional cycles. A spatial-based portfolio's risk-spreading property decreases with increasing regional cyclical agreement. Agreement increases with a less diverse mix of regional cycles and, by implication, less inter-regional trade. It also declines with decreasing asynchronicity between the (two) regions.

One would posit that if the UK market is dominated by node, that region and the rest of the nation would have similar cyclical properties. Relative to the reference cycle, the asynchronicity would be shorter and the correlation with the dominant region higher. In other words, the dominant region would be more 'attuned' to the reference series. However, with the smaller, peripheral region, distinctiveness will show up in terms of a lower correlation with the reference cycle.

Where the lead region is distinctive relative to the rest is of particular importance. If the lead region is distinctive, the logic of it being a driver of the reference cycle is problematic. The ripple effect implies price synchronisation after adjusting for a spatio-temporal lag.

References

Abbott, A., & De Vita, G. (2013). Testing for long-run convergence across regional house prices in the UK: A pairwise approach. *Applied Economics, 45*, 1227–1238.

Benito, A. (2006, March). How does the Down-Payment Constraint Affect the UK Housing Market (Bank of England Working Paper 294).

Canova, F. (1999). Does detrending matter for the determination of the reference cycle and the selection of turning point? *The Economic Journal, 109,* 125–150.

Carvalho, V., & Harvey, A. (2005). Growth, cycles and convergence in US regional time series. *International Journal of Forecasting, 21,* 667–686.

Chatfield, C. (1989). *The analysis of time series* (3rd ed.). Chapman and Hall: London.

Cogley, T., & Nason, J. (1995). Effects of the Hodrick-Pescott filter on trend and difference stationary time series: Implications for business cycle research. *Journal of Economic Dynamics and Control, 19,* 253–278.

Croux, C., Forni, M., & Reichlin, L. (2001). A measure of comovement for economic variables: Theory and empirics. *Review of Economics and Statistics, 83,* 232–241.

Dunn, R. (1983). Spectral analysis and distributed lags in geographical studies of local unemployment: 1. *Spectral and Cross Spectral Analysis, Environment and Planning A, 15,* 969–985.

Granger, C. (1969). Investigating causal relations by econometric models and cross-spectral methods. *Econometrica, 37,* 424–438.

Granger, C. (1988). Recent developments in a concept of causality. *Journal of Econometrics, 39,* 199–211.

Gray, D. (2013). House price diffusion: An application of spectral analysis to the prices of Irish second-hand dwellings. *Housing Studies, 28*(7), 869–890.

Gray, D. (2015). Hidden properties of Irish house price vintages. *Housing Studies, 30*(8), 1317–1353.

Guay, A., & St-Amant, P. (2005). Do the Hodrick-Pescott and Baxter King filters provide a good approximation of business cycles? *Annales D'Economie et de Statistique, 77,* 133–155.

Hamilton, J. (1994). *Time series analysis.* Princeton, NJ: Princeton University Press.

Harvey, A. (1993). *Time series models.* London: Harvester Wheatsheaf.

Harvey, A., & Trimbur, T. (2008). Trend estimation and the Hodrick-Prescott filter. *Journal of the Japan Statistical Society, 38*(1), 41–49.

Holmes, M. (2007). How convergent are regional house prices in the United Kingdom? Some new evidence from panel data unit root testing. *Journal of Economic and Social Research, 9*(1), 1–17.

Holmes, M., & Grimes, A. (2008). Is there long-run convergence among regional house prices in the UK? *Urban Studies, 45*(8), 1531–1544.

Hughes-Hallett, A., & Richter, C. (2004). Spectral analysis as a tool for financial policy: An analysis of the short-end of the British term structure. *Computational Economics, 23,* 271–288.

Igan, D., Kabundi, A., Nadal De Simine, F., Pinheiro, M., & Tamirisa, N. (2011). Housing, credit, and real activity cycles: Characteristics and comovements. *Journal of Housing Economics, 20,* 210–231.

King, R., & Rebelo, S. (1993). Low frequency filtering and real business cycles. *Journal of Economic Dynamics and Control, 17*(1–2), 207–231.

Kwiatkowski, D., Phillips, P. C. B., Scmidt, P., & Shin, Y. (1992). Testing the null hypothesis of stationarity against the alternative of a unit root. *Journal of Econometrics, 54,* 159–178.

Levy, D. (1994). Output, capital and labor in the short and long run. *Southern Economic Journal, 60*(4), 946–960.

Levy, D., & Dezhbakhshb, H. (2003). International evidence on output fluctuation and shock persistence. *Journal of Monetary Economics, 50,* 1499–1530.

Liow, K. (2007). Cycles and common cycles in real estate markets. *International Journal of Managerial Finance, 3*(3), 287–305.

Lütkepohl, H. (1982). Non-causality due to omitted variables. *Journal of Econometrics, 19,* 367–378.

Marchand, C. (1981). Maximum entropy spectra and the spatial and temporal dimensions of economic fluctuations in an urban system. *Geographical Analysis, 13,* 95–116.

Mayer, C. (1993). Taxes, income distribution, and the real estate cycle: Why all houses do not appreciate at the same rate. *New England Economic Review*, May/June, 39–50.

Meen, G. (1999). Regional house prices and the ripple effect: A new interpretation. *Housing Studies, 14*(6), 733–753.

Mundell, R. (1961). A theory of optimal currency areas. *American Economic Review, 51,* 657–664.

Pakko, M. (2000). The cyclical relationship between output and prices: An analysis in the frequency domain. *Journal of Money Credit and Banking, 32*(3), 382–399.

Park, H., & Fuller, W. (1995). Alternative estimators and unit root tests for the autoregressive process. *Journal of Time Series Analysis, 16,* 415–429.

Pesaran, M. H. (2007a). A pair-wise approach to testing for output and growth convergence. *Journal of Econometrics, 138,* 312–355.

Pesaran, M. H. (2007b). A simple panel unit root test in the presence of cross-section dependence. *Journal of Applied Econometrics, 22,* 265–312.

Phillips, P. C. B., & Jin, S. (2015). Business cycles, trend elimination, and the HP filter. Cowles Foundation Discussion Paper No. 2005, Yale University.
Rosenthal, L. (1986). Regional house price interactions in the UK, 1975–81: A cross-spectral analysis. *Applied Economics, 18,* 1011–1023.
Smith, B., & Tesarek, W. (1991). House prices and regional real estate cycles: Market adjustments in houston. *Real Estate Economics, 19*(3), 396–416.
Smith, K. (2001). Pre- and post-1987 crash frequency domain analysis among pacific rim equity markets. *Journal of Multinational Financial Management, 11*(1), 69–87.
Sommervoll, D., Borgersen, T.-A., & Wennemo, T. (2010). Endogenous housing market cycles. *Journal of Banking & Finance, 34*(3), 557–567.
Sun, J., Sim, L.-L., Hin, K., & Ho, D. (2007). The cyclical association of residential housing price and consumption. *Journal of Real Estate Portfolio Management, 13*(3), 219–248.
Tiller, R., & Bednazik, R. (1983). The behaviour of regional unemployment rates over time: Effects on dispersion and national unemployment. *Journal of Regional Science, 23,* 479–500.
Wang, P. (2003). *Financial econometrics: Methods and models.* London: Routledge.
Wilson, P., & Okunev, J. (1999). Spectral analysis of real estate and financial assets markets. *Journal of Property Investment and Finance, 17*(1), 61–74.
Witkiewicz, W. (2002). The use of the HP-filter in construction real estate cycle indicators. *Journal of Real Estate Research, 23,* 65–87.

5

House Price, Consumption, and Construction Data

Abstract This chapter reviews the data that is utilised, plus some used for context. Income and the consumption data are taken from the Quarterly National Accounts. Gross domestic product and household final consumption expenditure cover the period 1955Q1 to 2014Q4. The inflation rate is taken as the Retail Price Index. Secured and unsecured lending and household expenditure on consumer durables (CD) is available from datastream, for the second part of the data analysis. Quarterly house price data for the UK is taken from the Nationwide Building Society, covering the period from 1955Q1 to 2014Q4. The regional, vintage, and buyer group covers 32 years from 1983Q1.

Keywords Data analysis · House price data · Buyer · Household expenditure

5.1 Introduction

This section reviews the data that is utilised, plus some used for context. Income and the consumption data are taken from the Quarterly National Accounts. Gross domestic product (GDP) (YBHA) and household final

D. Gray, *Cycles in the UK Housing Economy*,
DOI 10.1007/978-3-319-63348-0_5

consumption expenditure, (HHE) (ABJQ), are taken from the ONS website, seasonally adjusted, at current prices, beginning in 1955Q1, which is taken from the ONS website. The latter does not include the purchase of houses or payment of interest on loans. Private expenditure on dwelling construction (MV6 M) is not seasonally adjusted. The inflation rate is taken as either the GDP deflator (MNF2) or the Retail Price Index (RPI). Secured and unsecured lending and household expenditure on consumer durables (CD) is available from datastream, but only for the shorter 32-year series.

Data on house purchase metrics is taken from the ONS: Housing Market, Table 29: simple average house prices, mortgage advances and incomes of borrowers, by new/other dwellings, type of buyer, and standard statistical region, from 1969 (previously DCLG Table 515).

Quarterly house price data for the UK is taken from the Nationwide Building Society, covering the period from 1955Q1 to 2014Q4. The regional, vintage, and buyer-group data cover 32 years from 1983Q1. Along with the Halifax Bank and based on its mortgage provision, the Nationwide provides a generally respected source of house price data, which is quoted widely in academic papers and by government agencies. On their website, the Nationwide discusses their methodology used when compiling the data. The data is based on approvals, not agreed sale prices, is survey based and is seasonally adjusted. Also, the quality of the dwelling could be changing over time: the mix of housing that is marketed could vary from year to year. To cater for this, the Nationwide makes adjustments for the quality mix variation. Although the Land Registry Index, a comprehensive source, is not survey based and reflects actual sales' prices, it is not mix-adjusted which made it more volatile (Thwaites and Wood 2003). In June 2016, a new official UK House Price Index (UK HPI) replaced house price indices published by the ONS and the Land Registry. Although the Land Registry index, a comprehensive source, is not survey-based and reflects actual sales' prices, it is not mix-adjusted, which adds some volatility (Thwaites and Wood, 2003). Like the Halifax and Nationwide, the UK HPI uses hedonic pricing adjusting for the mix of houses being sold in different periods by annually updating the fixed basket of properties. Although the Land Registry covers actual purchases rather than mortgage approvals, its repeat sales methodology, based on a standardised set of properties from

April 2000, only captures properties that are repurchased, ignoring any new build properties and under-representing properties that are seldom transacted. The Nationwide house price data has a most attractive property for spectral work, and the length of series (60 years) outstrips any other. The Nationwide's and Halifax's values represent a price of a typically transacted house. Both are based on mortgage approvals. The limitations are reviewed in Wood (2005) and Chandler and Disney (2014). If there are weaknesses in the data, these are more than outweighed by the benefits of the analysis, being able to expose cycles in very long series.

Northern Ireland is ignored as the risk–reward relationship may be coloured by sectarian issues; the Eire house price bubble was much larger than in the UK and overspilled to the province, and it has no common border with any other British region.

5.2 The Choice of Nominal Over Real Values

As an introduction to the consequences of filtering, there is a display of nominal values and a money deflator. Figure 5.1 covers long series of data comparing the cycle from the inflation index, the RPI, which is almost identical to GDP deflator, MNF2, and house prices and GDP. The setting for these using the H-P filter is 4700 (13 years).

Deflating any of the nominal series leads to change in slope, related to that inherent in the price deflation: however, what of the cycle? When generating the cyclical components in real terms, one might posit that the real cycles should be moderated. This turns out not to be the case. The real cycle is the nominal cycle minus the deflator. This has implications for the volatility of the variables concerned. If the cyclical element of inflation is out of synchronisation with the nominal variable it was meant to deflate, it would increase the volatility of the real value. From the axes in Fig. 5.1, the inflation cycle is less volatile than house prices. These results should be reflected in other metrics.

In Table 5.1, a measure of volatility, the standard deviation, is presented. In each of the three cases, the volatility increases. This issue is more important; the closer the volatility levels are relative to inflation, the greater the asynchronicity is.

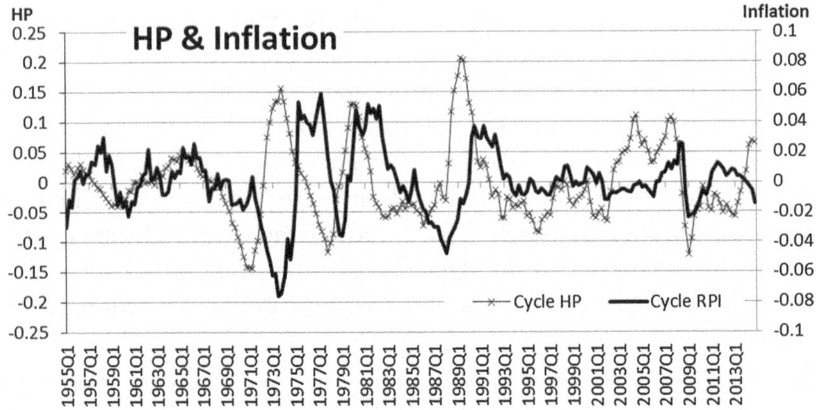

Fig. 5.1 Nominal house price cycle and inflation

Table 5.1 Real and nominal cycles

	Cycle	RPI	HHE	GDP	HP	HHEreal	GDPreal	HPreal
Standard deviation	10y	0.0179	0.0134	0.0158	0.0508	0.0163	0.0173	0.0566
	13y	0.0224	0.0175	0.0200	0.0640	0.0187	0.0200	0.0703
Correlation	10y		0.492	0.481	−0.161	−0.697	−0.599	−0.463
	13y		0.586	0.562	−0.118	−0.650	−0.560	−0.427

RPI Retail price index, *HHE* Household expenditure, *GDP* Gross domestic product, *HP* House price
Correlation with inflation

The correlation between inflation and three variables is displayed in Table 5.1 using a 10-and 13-year H-P filter. House prices are found to be notably out of phase relative to inflation. The other two switch from being pro-cyclical in nominal terms to counter-cyclical in real. The correlation values increase. House prices have a low correlation with inflation in nominal (−0.116) but high in real terms (−0.463) with the 10 year filter. This presents a problem for cyclical analysis. By injecting inflation into the cycle of the household expenditure and GDP the correlation of the real versions is 0.82 but 0.77 between the nominal with the 10 year filter but almost identical (.84) with the 13 year filter. In the frequency domain, this could be evident in the co-spectrum as a misleading cycle specifically related to inflation and not to the other two. Unlike trend, the nominal series' cycles do not appear to be subject to money effects, expanding with time. Moreover,

Madsen (2012) argues that buyers suffer from money illusion and many suggest price forecasts are at best myopic.

The cycle values are in logarithm form, so when added to the trend, they have a multiplicative effect, adding a proportion, not a value. As such, it will be presumed that the deflator of nominal variables is the de-trending of the series in logarithm form.

5.3 The Time Paths of Cycles and Trends

The parameter 1600 commonly applied to quarterly data. This is taken to remove the cyclical effects one would find in seasonal data. However, Harvey and Trimbur (2008) conclude that the H-P filter λ value acts as a 9.92-year high-pass filter with that value. Their use of a 32,000 value for a US investment cycle presumes a 21-year cycle. Phillips and Jin (2015) propose that the smoothing parameter should grow in relation to the sample size to address a standard criticism of the injection of spurious cycles; 1600 may be appropriate for 100 points but what of larger data series? Combining the two 30-year samples, the filter parameter is increased to 4700. This is not arbitrary. The 60 years' worth of quarterly data is de-trended using a 13-year filter. Aikman et al. (2014) find a 13⅓-year periodicity in credit. This is consistent with the other values discussed and with the eras of Meen (2011) and Scanlon and Whitehead (2011). In the longer run, the longer cycles in house prices and credit, which appear as trends when analysed over a few decades, could have common trends.

The resultant decompositions are displayed in Figs. 5.2 and 5.3. The trend lines, in natural log form, even with the 4700 setting, still contain long cycles. These longer cycles could be picked up by even higher settings. Agnello and Schuknecht (2011) use a 10,000 (15.7 years) H-P smoothing parameter to reveal an upward and a downward UK house price trend of seven years each, consistent with Bracke (2013) conclusions about long cycles.

The cyclical elements in Fig. 5.2 show the alignment of GDP and HHE. They vacillate closely together, but occasionally diverge. Construction and house prices have different trends, and the former

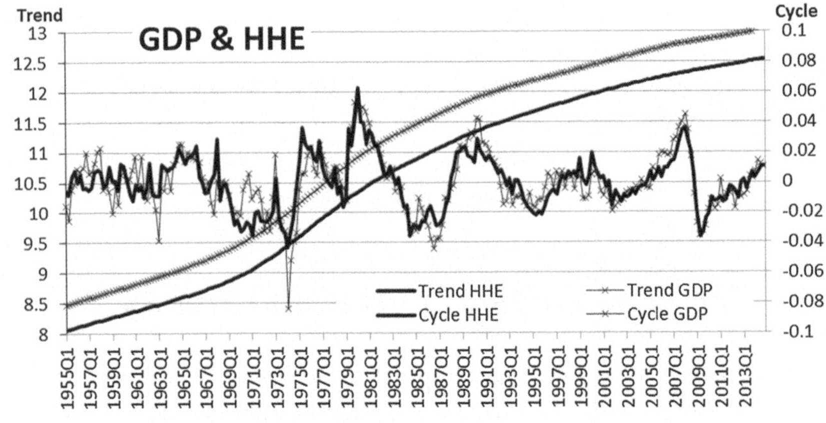

Fig. 5.2 Trend and cycle: GDP and household expenditure

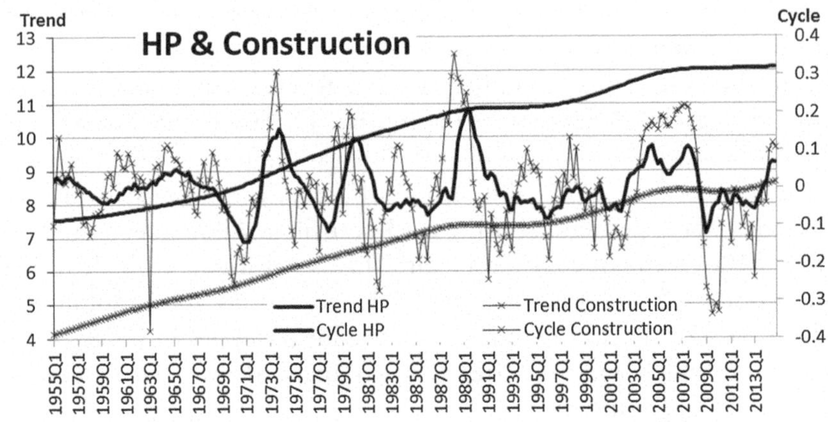

Fig. 5.3 Trend and cycle: house prices and construction expenditure

is more volatile than the latter. The most violent drops in construction occur around the times of house price collapses in 1973, 1988, and 2007, which is consistent with Leamer and DiPasquale and Wheaton discussion of construction and price cycles.

Figures 5.4 and 5.5 provide images of lending and consumption by type. Secured lending and non-durables have greater levels but lower volatilities compared with unsecured and consumer durables.

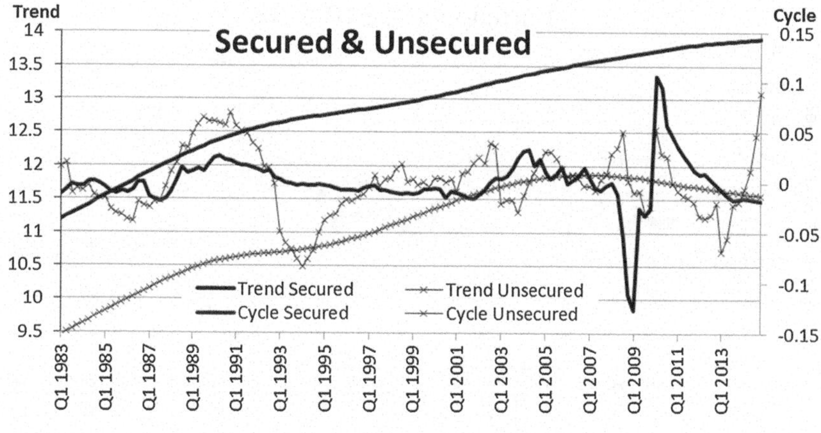

Fig. 5.4 Trend and cycle: secured and unsecured lending

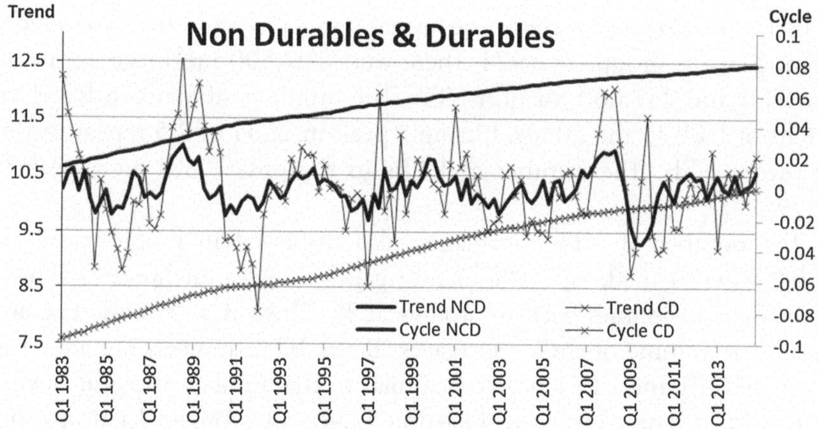

Fig. 5.5 Trend and cycle: consumer durables and non-durables expenditure

5.4 Buyer-Group Prices

To provide some buyer-group context, Fig. 5.6 shows numbers of buyers by type of mortgagee. The numbers of FTBs in the market are at local maxima in 1977/1979, 1986/1988, 1994, 1999, and 2006. For RB, the corresponding years are 1979, 1988, 1993, and 2004, which

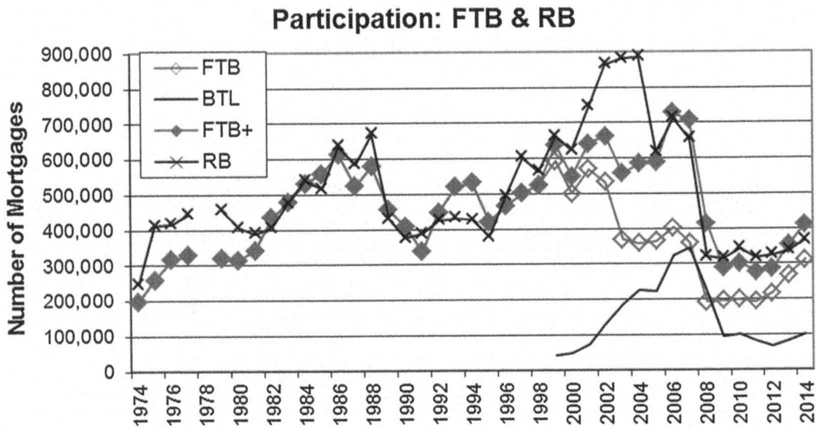

Fig. 5.6 Number of mortgage approvals by buyer group

coincide less regularly than one might expect if the buyers formed a homogeneous group. In 1974, there were 197,500 mortgage approvals for FTB and 247,000 for non-FTB. The numbers of loans to RB deviate from FTB in the 2000s, hitting a peak in 2004 of 2.5 repeat buyers for every FTB. The number of FTBs in the post-1980s hit a peak in 1999.

The number of BTL mortgages, also displayed in profile, peaks in 2008, when it made up 30% of mortgage advances for house purchase. After that, it declines back to around 12%. There is a dramatic rise and fall in the volume of these mortgages. If the BTL numbers are added to those of FTB, the FTB+ profile is similar to the number of repeat buyers. The ratio of repeat buyers to first-time buyers plus buy-to-let drops to a maximum of 1.5 to one, slightly above the ratio in 1979. The numbers of advances for FTB and RB are positively correlated (0.57); if FTB+ and RB are considered, it points to a close association (0.83). The RB and FTB may be jointly dependent on common financial policies, or the RB is dependent on the FTB providing funding for their next move (Fig. 5.7).

Björlund and Söderland (1999) argue that the LTI can mirror the state of a property cycle. Using Swedish data, they find a drift in the LTI, which is an indicator of a property bubble. In Figs. 5.7 and 5.8, Council of Mortgage Lenders' Regulated Mortgage Survey data indicate

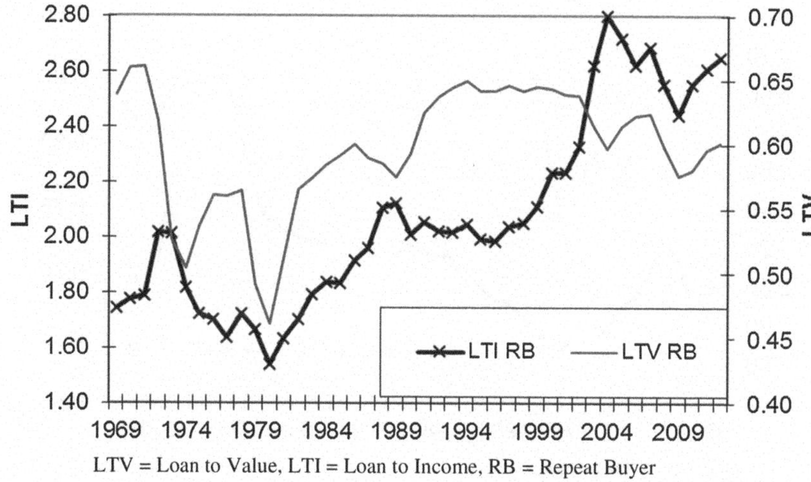

Fig. 5.7 RB purchasing metrics

that the loan to value (LTV) for the purchase of dwellings by non-first-time buyers [or RBs] fluctuates from 0.45 to 0.65. Loan to income (LTI) has a minimum in 1980, but, in the liberalisation era, there is an upward trend more or less from then on. If one were to look for local peaks in the LTI, one might highlight three (1973, 1989, and 2004), each preceded a housing crash, and the gaps would be around 16 years. The LTV troughs (1974, 1980, 1989, 2004, and 2009) would suggest a different driver or a cycle at a higher frequency, with gaps of around 5–9 years. The data show variations in the LTV and an upward trend in the LTI ratios, so that a repeat buyer could borrow 2.6 times the value of their income at the end of the era, approaching double what they could in 1980, assuming income remained constant.

The profile for FTBs is similar to RB. The key difference is that the values for LTV are much higher, reflecting the equity that RBs have in their dwellings (Fig. 5.7).

Table 5.2 reports the minimum FTB dwelling price during the 32 years, which is £20,801, around £10,000 less than that for an RB's abode. The corresponding values for the maximum values are £162,856 and £53,000. If the maximum is divided by the minimum, FTB prices

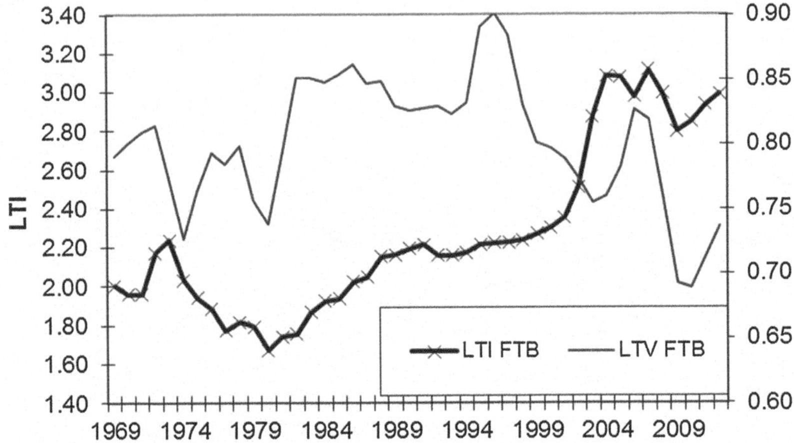

FTB = First Time Buyers

Fig. 5.8 FTB purchasing metrics

Table 5.2 Buyer-group price growth

	FTB	FTB*	RB	RB*
Maximum	£162,856	£154,416	£215,120	£205,714
Minimum	£20,801	£20,429	£30,399	£29,901
Range	£142,046	£133,987	£184,721	£175,813
Ratio	7.826	7.559	7.077	6.880
Standard deviation		0.051		0.046

*Trend element only

grew by 7.83 times, whereas RB rose by 7.08 times. Separating the trend element only, the picture does not change. An asterisk identifies the corresponding figures. In other words, rather than becoming disconnected over the period, FTB prices narrowed the gap.

The standard deviation of the cyclical element suggests the FTB prices are more volatile than those of RBs. The standard deviation of annual FTB house price growth, estimated by Bentio over the period from 1985 to 2003, is 8.5%, and for RB, it is 9.6%, consistent with OMR. However, the H-P-filtered price data, which has very similar undulations to Bentio's house price inflation profile, proffers a standard deviation of 5.05% for the same period using quarterly data for FTB and 4.59% for RB. Over the same period, the trend extracted by the H-P 1600 filter saw an annual growth rate of 6.52% as opposed to 6.21% for RB.

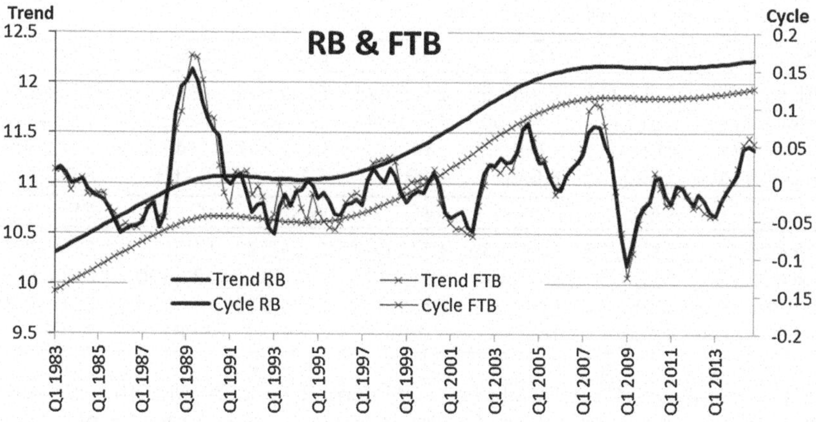

Fig. 5.9 Trends and cycles in house prices: RB and FTB

The trends and cycles extracted by the H-P filter for FTB and RB using a 10-year filter are displayed in Fig. 5.9. The high-pass filter appears to leave a long cycle in the trend of possibly 15 years in both series appearing as common trends in the house price series. Although the two smoothed price lines appear to run in parallel, there are periods of convergence and divergence over time. Since 1995, there appears to be a convergence of prices. Although consistent with the higher growth rate in Table 5.2, this is unexpected.

Turning points in the price and participation cycles give a benchmark to the 1989 and 2008 house price crises. The peaks for both FTB and RB prices are 1989Q2 and 2007Q3. Note that for both RB and FTB market participation in Fig. 5.6 peaks before prices in Fig. 5.9, suggesting affordability filters out buyers from both groups. The one-year gap for the former crisis is extended to a three-year gap in the case of the RBs. As expected, this is less than seven for FTB, but the flat buyer's participation is likely to be shortened by the entry of the BTL buyer.

The violent swings in house prices observed by Levin and Price (2009) are particularly evident in the precipitous changes in 1989/1990 and 2007/2008. The cyclical element suggests amplitude of around ±3% trend in Fig. 5.6. However, in 1989 and 2008, there were violent changes of around 15% of the price. In both cases, the FTB

Table 5.3 Regional price growth: RB

RB	N	YH	NW	EM	WM	EA
Price high	£149,312	£164,169	£172,423	£170,354	£178,467	£203,989
Price low	£26,711	£24,780	£29,064	£27,507	£28,957	£30,481
Difference	£122,601	£139,389	£143,359	£142,847	£149,509	£173,509
Growth rate	5.590	6.625	5.932	6.193	6.163	6.692
	OMET	LON	SW	WA	SC	OSE
Price high	£324,203	£437,439	£223,063	£164,347	£156,311	£251,466
Price low	£43,471	£42,667	£31,248	£28,431	£31,380	£35,013
Difference	£280,732	£394,772	£191,815	£135,915	£124,932	£216,454
Growth rate	7.458	10.252	7.139	5.780	4.981	7.182

EA East Anglia, *EM* East Midlands, *LON* Central London, *N*North, *NW* North West, *OMET* Outer Metropolitan London, *OSE* Outer South East, *SC* Scotland, *SW* South West, *WA* Wales, *WM* West Midlands, *YH* Yorkshire/Humberside

Table 5.4 Regional price growth: FTB

FTB	N	YH	NW	EM	WM	EA
Price high	£99,567	£112,355	£113,199	£124,596	£127,628	£147,782
Price low	£22,073	£18,820	£16,785	£15,973	£16,738	£19,579
Difference	£77,493	£93,534	£96,414	£108,623	£110,890	£128,203
Growth rate	4.511	5.970	6.744	7.800	7.625	7.548
	OMET	LON	SW	WA	SC	OSE
Price high	£222,095	£330,163	£164,681	£119,328	£104,290	£176,247
Price low	£28,685	£31,349	£22,397	£18,334	£19,705	£23,571
Difference	£193,410	£298,813	£142,285	£100,994	£84,585	£152,676
Growth rate	7.743	10.532	7.353	6.508	5.293	7.477

fall was greater than that seen for RB. Of course, in absolute terms, the change was larger for RB.

Over the 32 years, house prices from 1983 regional house prices increased at a rapid rate but not all in-line with the UK. Table 5.3 reports four regions outshone the UK (the South West, Outer South East, Outer Metropolitan and London). London's repeat buyer prices grew by a factor of 10.252, over twice a rapid and the slowest growing region, Scotland (4.98). The level values for the first-time buyer in Table 5.4 are lower, but the growth rates are higher in all but the North and Yorkshire-Humberside.

Table 5.5 Regional price growth: vintages

	New	Modern	Old
Price high	£187,588	£165,157	£184,521
Price low	£34,064	£26,319	£22,651
Difference	£153,524	£138,838	£161,870
Growth rate	5.507	6.275	8.146
Standard deviation	0.043	0.046	0.049

House price vintages show very different growth rates. *Old* grew far more rapidly than Modern or *New* and had the greatest volatility. As *Old* dwellings were not the most expensive, this set of results is unexpected (Table 5.5).

References

Agnello, L., & Schuknecht, L. (2011). Booms and busts in housing markets: Determinants and implications. *Journal of Housing Economics, 20*(4), 171–190.

Aikman, D., Haldane, A., & Nelson, B. (2014). Curbing the credit cycle. *The Economic Journal, 125*(June), 1072–1109.

Björlund, K., & Söderland, B. (1999). Property cycles speculative bubbles and the gross income multiplier. *Journal of Real Estate Research, 18*(1), 151–174.

Bracke, P. (2013). How long to housing cycles last? A duration analysis for 19 OECD countries. *Journal of Housing Economics, 22,* 213–230.

Chandler, D., & Disney, R. (2014). *Measuring house prices: A comparison of different indices* (Briefing Note BN146). Institute of Fiscal Studies. https://www.ifs.org.uk/bns/bn146.pdf. Accessed 8 May 2017.

Harvey, A., & Trimbur, T. (2008). Trend estimation and the Hodrick-Prescott filter. *Journal of the Japan Statistical Society, 38*(1), 41–49.

Levin, E., & Price, G. (2009). What determines the price elasticity of house supply? Real Interest Rate Effects and Cyclical Asymmetries. *Housing Studies, 24*(6), 713–736.

Madsen, J. (2012) A behavioural model of house prices, *Journal of Economics Behavior & Organization, 82*, 21–38.

Meen, G. (2011). The economic consequences of mortgage debt. *Journal of Housing and the Build Environment, 26*(3), 263–276.

Phillips, P. C. B., & Jin, S. (2015). *Business cycles, trend elimination, and the HP filter* (Cowles Foundation Discussion Paper No. 2005), Yale University.

Scanlon, K., & Whitehead, C. (2011). The UK mortgage market: Responding to volatility. *Journal of Housing and the Build Environment, 26*, 277–293.

Thwaites, G., & Wood, R. (2003). The measurement of house prices. *Bank of England Quarterly Bulletin, 43*(1), 38–46.

Wood, R. (2005). A comparison of UK residential house price indices. In *Bank for International Settlements, Real Estate Indicators and Financial Stability*, Bank of International Settlement (Vol. 21, pp. 212–227). https://www.bis.org/publ/bppdf/bispap21.htm. Accessed 8 May 2017.

6
Evidence of Cycles in the Housing Economy

Abstract In this chapter, there is a consideration of five groups of data. The long series covers 60 years. That data is divided and each half is compared with the other for notable changes. A third set involves regional house prices; a fourth set covers buyer types; and the fifth considers house vintage.

Keywords Regional house prices · Buyer types · House vintage · House prices

6.1 Introduction

There is a consideration of five groups of data. The long series covers 60 years. That data is divided, and each half is compared with the other for notable changes. A third set involves regional house prices. A fourth set covers buyer types, and the fifths considers house vintage.

D. Gray, *Cycles in the UK Housing Economy*,
DOI 10.1007/978-3-319-63348-0_6

6.2 Capturing Longer Cycles in Long Series

Calderon and Fuentes (2014) identify a 7½-year cycle in UK GDP. Levy and Dezhbakhsh (2003) show single peak at around 6–8 years. Using annual data, 12% of the variance is accounted for in low frequencies, with 70% in among the business cycles. The power spectra for GDP and household expenditure are displayed. Figure 6.1 as follows: 30 years to 1 year plus the long run, zero frequency. Peaks in the GDP series occur at 10- and 5.45-year cycles. Including these two and all frequencies in between, these business cycles account for 35% of all variance. A further 29% is accounted for in lower frequencies. The peak in the HHE power spectrum is at the 10- and 15-year cycles. In this range, 36% of the total variance is accounted for. Longer cycles account for a further 10%. Consumption is spread over a range of long frequencies. As indicated in Fig. 6.2, the two series are most closely aligned at the 10-year cycle.

Using GDP as a proxy for the business cycle, the longer run points to a 10-year cycle. Given the filter is set for 13 years, what would be

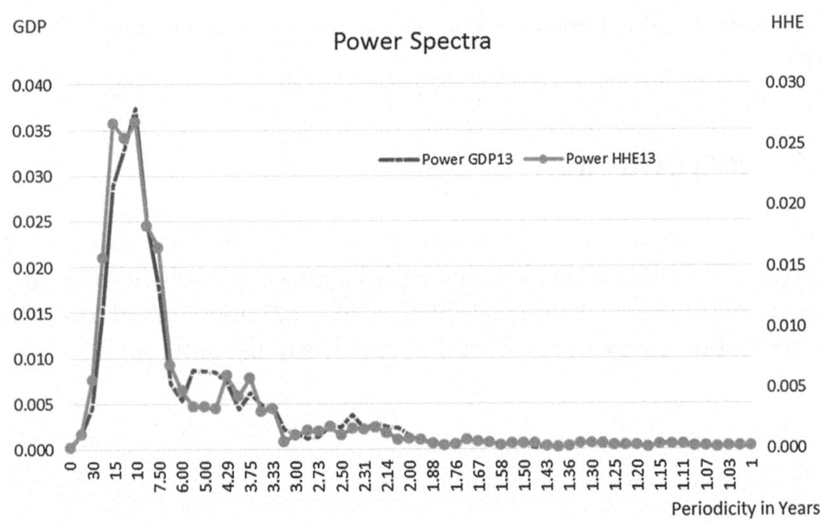

Fig. 6.1 Power spectra GDP and HHE

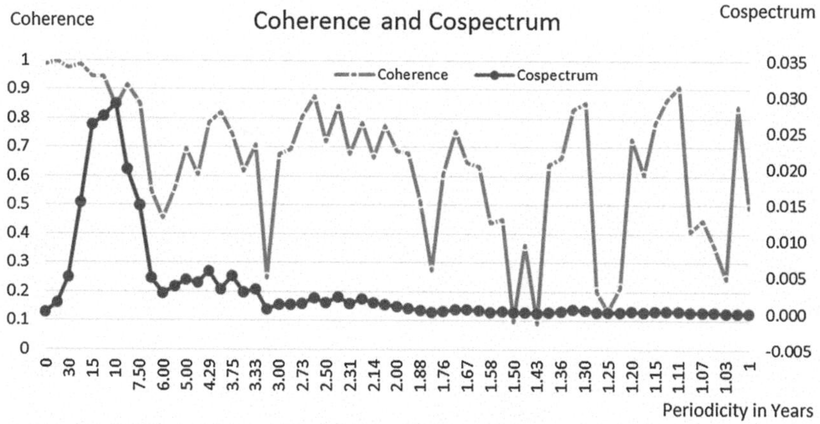

Fig. 6.2 Coherence and cospectrum GDP and HHE

allocated to the trend is attributed to the cyclical element, so boosting the values in the longer cycles, relative to the 10-year filter. This suggests that a H-P setting of 1600 may lead to key cycles being ignored.

The peak in the house price spectrum occurs at the 7½ with a minor peak at 15-year cycle and a further small, but important one at 5.45 years. In this range, 70% of the total variance is accounted for. Longer cycles account for a further 6.7%. Dicks (1989) postulates a system where there is a 7-year lag between moves that predicts broadly the 'right' number of repeat buyers in the market which could explain this cycle. As indicated in Fig. 6.4, the cospectrum highlights the three cycles mentioned as those of note. Of particular interest is the 5.45-year cycle where there is a negative relationship between house prices and consumption (Fig. 6.3).

The values in Table 6.1 reflect the figures above. Gain can be interpreted as the regression coefficient in the time domain. To generate the equivalent of a beta value in regression, the gain values are adjusted by the standard deviation of both filtered series. The adjusted gain value at the 10-year cycle is interpreted as the impact of a change of one standard deviation in income results in 0.886 × one standard deviation in household consumption expenditure. Given that income volatility is

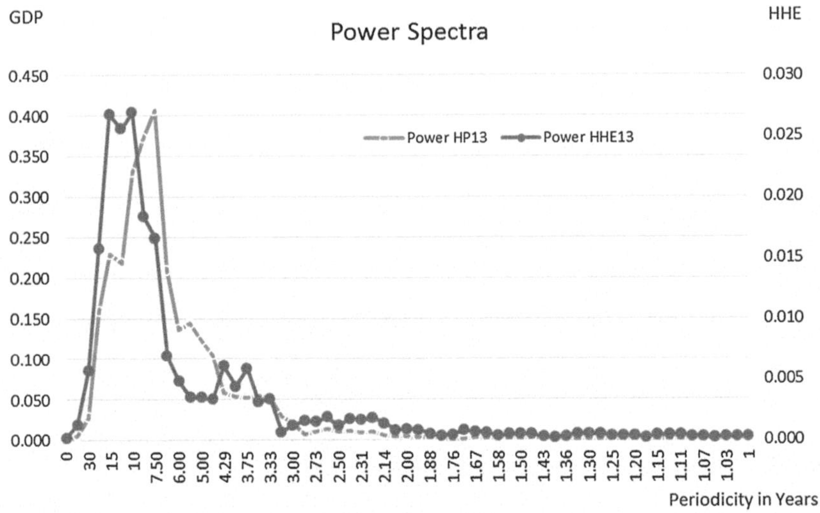

Fig. 6.3 Power spectra house prices and HHE

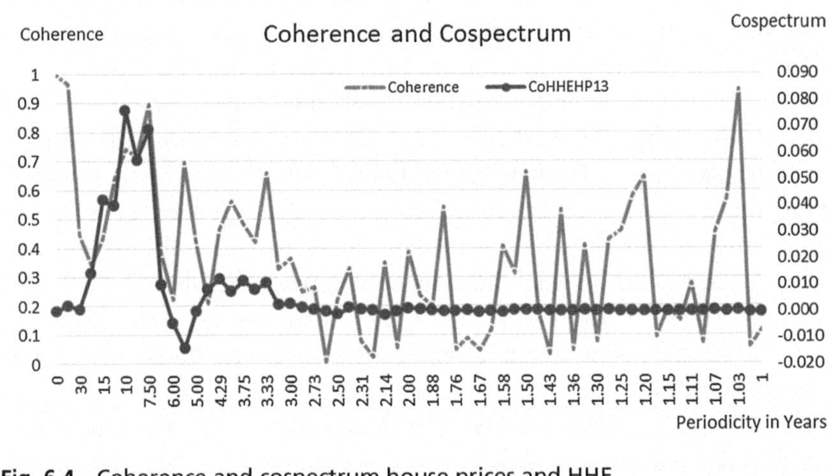

Fig. 6.4 Coherence and cospectrum house prices and HHE

accommodated, a value below one implies that there is smoothing, as the PIH suggests.

In his discussion of the PIH, Hoover (2012) points out that the aggregation of the individual to the economy, the age distribution of the

Table 6.1 Spectral characteristics, long series

Cycle	Power spectrum		Phase	Adjusted gain		Coherence		Co-Spectrum	Coh	Sync
	HHE	HP	Qtrs	HHE to HP	HP to HHE	Coh^2	Sync^2			
15	**0.027**	0.229	5.9	0.528	0.823	0.289	0.146	0.042	0.537	0.382
12	0.026	0.218	6.4	0.64	1.001	0.287	0.353	0.040	0.536	0.594
10	**0.027**	0.331	2.2	0.827	0.895	**0.653**	0.087	**0.076**	0.808	0.296
8.57	0.018	0.372	3.3	1.042	0.685	0.483	0.231	0.057	0.695	0.48
7.50	0.017	**0.406**	2.3	1.283	0.697	**0.706**	**0.188**	0.069	0.84	0.434
5.45	0.004	0.144	8.4	1.46	0.477	0.398	0.298	**−0.014**	−0.631	0.546
		GDP	Weeks	HHE to GDP	GDP to HHE					
15	**0.027**	0.029	−32.4	0.886	1.069	**0.884**	**0.063**	0.026	0.94	−0.251
12	0.026	0.033	−26.3	0.969	0.975	**0.880**	**0.065**	0.027	0.938	−0.255
10	**0.027**	**0.037**	−5.5	0.947	0.886	0.835	0.004	**0.029**	0.914	−0.061
8.57	0.018	0.025	15.5	0.975	0.94	**0.874**	0.043	0.020	0.935	0.208
7.50	0.017	0.018	20.4	0.837	1.016	0.762	0.088	0.015	0.873	0.297
5.45	0.004	0.009	−21.2	1.027	0.544	0.444	0.114	0.004	0.666	−0.338

Bold highlights greatest values

populous matters. The young and elderly dissave whilst the middle-aged are paying off debt or are saving. Muellbauer (2007) posits that there is an aggregate consumption effect due to the down payment a FTB must make. Forced to sacrifice greater current consumption expenditure to find the growing down payment, the first-time buyer is disadvantaged by rising house prices. The down-trader, by contrast, can extract equity to boost their consumption. The first-time buyer sacrifice is posited by Muellbauer to outweigh the last time seller benefit, so, as prices rise consumption may fall. He suggests that this negative house price effect occurs in unsophisticated credit markets and would be reduced in a less credit-constrained era. Renters are also affected. Sheiner (1995) finds that the down payment is a prime motivation for saving. As such, HHE will be reduced with house price increases. Such a negative relationship is evident at the 5½-year cycle in Fig. 6.4, suggesting there is a small effect on consumption at this cycle.

The phase values indicate that house prices lead consumption by 30 weeks at the 7½-year cycle and over two years at the 5½-year cycle, a long delay relative to the cycle. HHE leads GDP at the 10-year cycle by 5½ weeks.

A standard debate concerns the impact of house prices on consumption. The adjusted gain suggests that, at the 10-year cycle, household expenditure is as sensitive to house prices as it is to GDP. However, at the key 7½-year housing cycle, the adjusted gain is much lower. The wealth effect from housing, one would expect, should affect consumption at this cycle, implying that a paper increase in wealth due to house prices does not have a notable wealth effect.

6.3 Consumption, Income and Housing—What Has Changed?

6.3.1 HHE and GDP

Over a 30-year period from 1955 to 1984, using a 10-year filter, there are two peaks in the GDP. The first is at 6 and the second at 4.29 years. Consumption is spread over a wide range of cycles from 4.29 to 10 years, which is indicative of a dislocation between consumption and income. The adjusted gain show relatively low values consistent with smoothing of consumption.

Over a second 30-year period from 1985 to 2014, for GDP there is a range of high values in the 10–6 year range, with the peak occurring around 7½ years. The business cycle, as indicated by GDP, has been extended, or at least the most prominent peak has altered. Consumption follows the same pattern as income, which is again a change compared with the earlier era. With both of these periods, there are peaks in the range highlighted by Levy and Dezhbakhsh (2003). Indeed, Calderon and Fuentes' (2014) 7½ years is confirmed.

The values reported in Table 6.2 suggest income and consumption have lengthened cycles. The cohesion values for the first 30 years are lower than the second implying co-movement has intensified. There is support from adjusted gain, where the values increase across the two eras. Indeed, the first era seems out of line with the other two. This latter point is considered further. Using a Smith (2001) test, there is a consideration of whether the liberalisation of finance changed consumption relative to income in the second 30 years compared with the first. A null of no change in coherence is not rejected (Wilcoxon Signed Ranks $Z = -0.614$ [0.539]). Indeed, the same procedure on the squared cohesion and squared synchronicity also indicates no change (−1.634 [0.102], −1.185 [0.236]). Liberalisation did not intensify or weaken the link between income and HHE. HHE leads GDP by a matter of 3 weeks in the first era at the 6-year cycle, but lag by 9 weeks in the second, perhaps indicating greater borrowing-funded consumption.

6.3.2 HHE and House Prices

The house price power spectrum also has altered. In Table 6.3, volatility appears to be lower and the key cycle appears to have lengthened to 10 years. The first-time buyer sacrifice may be evident at the 5-year cycle in the first 30-year period where the cohesion value is negative. This disappears in the second 30 years, consistent with the Muellbauer and the liberalisation of mortgage finance in that second period.

Table 6.2 Spectral characteristics, short series GDP HHE

Cycle	Power spectrum		Phase	Adjusted gain		Coherence		Co-Spectrum	Coh	Sync
	GDP	HHE	Weeks	HHE to GDP	GDP to HHE	Coh^2	Sync^2			
10	0.0076	**0.0069**	3.7	0.719	0.873	0.626	0.001	0.0057	0.791	0.035
7.5	0.0062	0.0054	−3.1	0.638	0.749	0.477	0.001	0.0040	0.691	−0.035
6	**0.0118**	**0.0069**	−2.6	0.899	0.706	0.633	0.002	**0.0072**	0.796	−0.041
5	0.0095	0.0066	−17.7	0.864	0.798	0.571	0.119	0.0060	0.755	−0.344
4.29	**0.0128**	**0.0067**	−10.7	1.043	0.731	0.695	0.067	**0.0077**	0.834	−0.260
10	0.0102	**0.0072**	21.0	0.932	1.023	0.893	0.060	0.0081	0.945	0.245
7.5	**0.0132**	**0.0076**	9.3	0.979	0.872	0.835	0.019	**0.0091**	0.914	0.137
6	0.0115	0.0067	5.5	0.916	0.824	0.746	0.009	0.0076	0.864	0.097
5	0.0057	0.0021	−15.2	1.079	0.617	0.580	0.086	0.0027	0.761	−0.293
4.29	0.0032	0.0025	9.7	0.743	0.882	0.607	0.048	0.0022	0.779	0.218

Bold highlights greatest values

Upper section 1955–1984, *lower section* 1985–2014

Table 6.3 Spectral characteristics, short series HP HHE

Cycle	Power spectrum		Phase	Adjusted gain		Coherence		Co-Spectrum	Coh	Sync
	HHE	HP	Qtrs	HHE to HP	HP to HHE	Coh^2	Sync^2			
10	**0.0069**	0.126	3.3	0.767	0.526	0.304	0.099	**0.0162**	0.552	0.315
7.5	0.0054	**0.254**	5.3	1.435	0.386	0.11	0.444	0.0123	0.332	0.666
6	**0.0069**	0.25	4.35	1.243	0.433	0.095	0.443	0.0128	0.308	0.666
5	0.0066	0.157	5.15	0.942	0.494	0.001	0.464	−0.001	−0.033	0.681
4.29	**0.0067**	0.053	−0.9	0.183	0.29	0.048	0.006	0.0041	0.218	−0.074
10	**0.0072**	**0.112**	4.31	0.812	0.941	0.464	0.3	**0.0194**	0.681	0.548
7.5	**0.0076**	0.08	3.27	0.682	1.164	0.477	0.318	0.017	0.69	0.564
6	0.0067	**0.102**	1.96	0.616	0.733	0.343	0.109	0.0153	0.585	0.33
5	0.0021	0.076	−1.41	1.009	0.507	0.418	0.094	0.0082	0.646	−0.306
4.29	0.0025	**0.087**	−0.01	0.952	0.483	0.46	0	0.0099	0.678	−0.002

Bold highlights greatest values
Upper section 1955–1984, *lower section* 1985–2014

Attanasio et al. (2011) note that, over the 40 years from the early 1970s, large increases in house prices were mirrored by consumption booms. Large busts followed these. The correlation of the growth of the two was reported as 0.74. Gain values from house prices to consumption in the second era are larger than in the first. Cohesion and cospectrum values also increased. Indeed, in the second era, at the 7½- and 6-year cycles, there are symptoms of a strong wealth effect which are not there in the first era. That said, a null of no change in coherence is not rejected (Z = −0.528 [0.598]). Indeed, the same procedure on the squared cohesion and squared synchronicity also indicates no change (−0.794 [0.427], −0.513 [0.608]).

To summarise, the business cycle became longer. Campbell and Mankiw (1991) posit that in a less credit-constrained era, consumption is free(r) to move towards that level associated with permanent income. The consumption horizon may have lengthened suggesting a greater concentration in the longer frequencies. Cutler asserts there would be a stronger link between house prices and consumption expenditure in the financially liberalised era. Although there is a closer relationship, this is not supported here, statistically.

6.4 Construction Expenditure

6.4.1 The Long View

Barras and Ferguson (1985) find a major and a minor cycle for almost all the UK property construction series they examine. For example, there is a 6½-year cycle major, a 15-quarter minor cycle in private housing construction, and a 9-year periodicity in private commercial property construction commissioning. Construction expenditure power spectrum in Fig. 6.4 indicates two peaks, echoing Barras and Ferguson (1985). The two concerned, at 8.6, and 5-year cycles, do not align with prices. The coherence peaks (7½- and 5-year cycles) come from each of the power spectra. The phase values in Table 6.4 point to a lead of Construction Expenditure over House Prices of around 2.3–3.3 quarters. If these

Table 6.4 Spectral characteristics, long series HP construction

Cycle	Power spectrum		Phase	Adjusted gain		Coherence		Co-Spectrum	Coh	Sync
	HP	Const	Qtrs	HP to Const	Const to HP	Coh^2	$Sync^2$			
15.00	0.2291	0.412	1.68	0.590	1.300	0.743	0.024	0.265	0.862	0.154
12.00	0.2177	0.731	−0.44	0.639	0.755	0.481	0.002	0.277	0.694	−0.040
10.00	0.3307	0.949	3.67	0.590	0.816	0.339	0.143	0.326	0.582	0.379
8.57	0.3723	**1.043**	2.35	0.605	0.856	0.427	0.090	0.407	0.654	0.301
7.50	**0.4063**	0.831	2.65	0.639	1.239	**0.573**	**0.219**	**0.440**	0.757	0.468
6.67	0.2087	0.318	0.95	0.411	1.069	0.418	0.022	0.167	0.646	0.147
6.00	0.1364	0.578	4.01	0.793	0.742	0.146	0.442	0.107	0.383	0.665
5.45	0.1436	0.639	4.05	0.883	0.788	0.107	0.589	0.099	0.327	0.767
5.00	0.1229	**0.910**	3.34	1.332	0.714	**0.236**	**0.715**	0.162	0.486	0.846
4.62	0.1048	0.618	2.24	1.042	0.701	0.383	0.348	0.157	0.619	0.590

Bold highlights greatest values

were building 'starts', that would confound the expected causation: DiPasquale and Wheaton's myopic model predicts the reverse causation. The synchronicity indicates suggest that, at a 5-year cycle, construction is notably out of phase with prices, consistent with a leading or speculative attribute of dwelling investment (Fig. 6.5).

The gain values in Fig. 6.6 are interpreted as illustrating increasing price elasticity of housing supply with time. Consistent with Masden (2012), the declining gain values from Construction to Prices suggest the supply has a long but not a short horizon effect. The rising gain from house price to Construction suggests building starts are affected by short-run price effects.

6.4.2 Evidence of a Change?

Table 6.5 indicates that Construction over the two 30-year periods changes its profile, with a lengthening of the key cycle from 5 to 7½ years. The full 60 years featuring both suggests a shift of emphasis from one cycle to the other. In Table 6.3, house price volatility appears to be

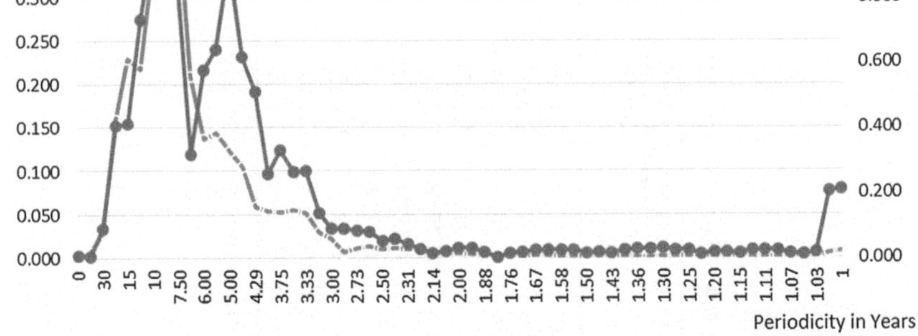

Fig. 6.5 Power spectra house prices and construction

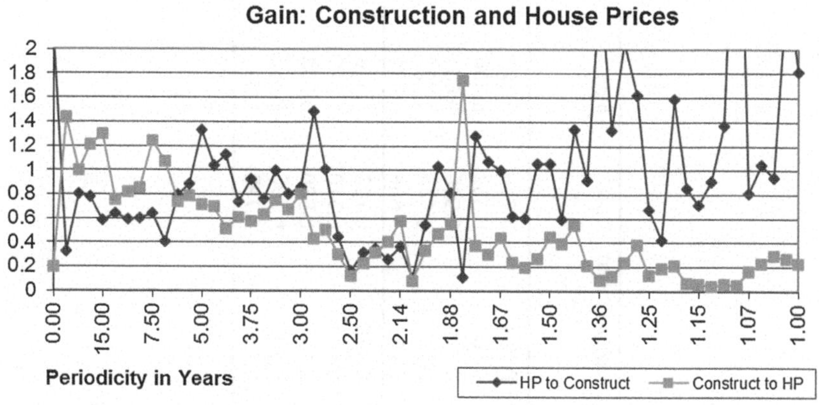

Fig. 6.6 Gain construction and house prices

lower and the key cycle appears to have lengthened to 10 years. There has been a greater emphasis on longer cycles in the second era across four variables examined.

The increasing price elasticity of supply with horizon is evident in the first period but not the second. In this latter period, the horizon does not seem to affect price sensitivity in the manner normally expected. The Barker (2003) report highlights vested interests in maintaining low output among Local Authorities, homeowners and builders. The planning process is restrictive and insensitive to price signals. The industry itself acts to restrict supply of new builds to manage price volatility but is also short of skilled workers, which also constrains construction.

DiPasquale and Wheaton's myopic price model predicts cycles of building and pricing such that construction sector would build sufficient houses to drive prices down. A positive relationship at both cycles could be explained by a weak output response to price, which has been a feature of UK housing (Meen 2000). The cospectrum values in Table 6.4 indicate a lack of an inverse relationship, suggesting that excess supply of new dwellings is not a common feature of the UK's housing market. As such, cycle turning points are not explained in DiPasquale and Wheaton's terms. An alternative explanation for a collapse in house prices in the UK could rely on other factors, most likely among them is unaffordability of mortgage payments. Perhaps

Table 6.5 Spectral characteristics, short series HP construction

Cycle	Power spectrum		Phase	Adjusted gain		Coherence		Co-Spectrum	Coh	Sync
	HP	Const	Qtrs	HP to Const	Const to HP	Coh^2	$Sync^2$			
10.00	0.1256	0.051	1.01	0.266	2.443	0.634	0.016	0.063	0.796	0.127
7.50	**0.2544**	0.352	3.95	0.499	1.333	0.304	0.360	0.165	0.552	0.600
6.00	0.2499	0.425	3.45	0.588	1.277	0.287	0.463	**0.175**	0.536	0.681
5.00	0.1571	**0.467**	2.96	0.815	1.012	**0.296**	**0.529**	0.147	0.544	0.727
4.29	0.0533	0.348	2.20	1.164	0.658	0.367	0.399	0.083	0.606	0.631
10.00	**0.1119**	0.501	2.64	0.674	0.913	0.516	0.100	**0.170**	0.718	0.316
7.50	0.0800	**0.726**	3.75	0.900	0.601	0.270	0.271	0.125	0.520	0.520
6.00	**0.1015**	0.585	2.93	0.785	0.825	0.336	0.312	0.141	0.580	0.558
5.00	0.0758	0.522	2.89	0.879	0.775	0.258	0.423	0.101	0.508	0.650
4.29	**0.0869**	0.300	1.53	0.711	1.248	**0.637**	**0.251**	0.129	0.798	0.501

Bold highlights greatest values
Upper section 1955–1984, *lower section* 1985–2014

the so-called Minsky point is passed, where mortgage interest payments cannot be met. If supply places less of a downwards force on prices in a Minskyan world, it could herald an era of a larger bubble.

Although squared cohesion does increase (−3.272, [0.001]), the Smith (2001) approach suggests a null of no change in coherence is not rejected (Z = −1.641 [0.101]).

6.5 How Is Lending Affected by the Housing Economy?

6.5.1 Lending and GDP

A further consideration, but only in the second 30 years concerns secured and unsecured lending. It is argued that rising prices and rising incomes both allow borrowers to access more mortgage finance. Rising house prices though should disadvantage the first-time buyer. However, relaxed lending should drive house purchases and demand. Meen (2000) implies a credit cycle should induce price cycles of the same periodicities, with relatively strong associations. By contrast, Chen et al. (2004) argue that monetary cycles tend to correspond with increased demand in the housing market. If so, credit should follow house price inflation, accommodating demand. Aikman et al. (2014) suggest that UK loans or credit provision is pro-cyclical, with amplitude twice that of the general business cycle, as proxied by real GDP, but a periodicity that is twice as long as the one for GDP. Moreover, they find a minor cycle of 4½-years in duration. That said, they find variations in GDP do not account much for perturbations in credit.

Drehmann et al. (2012) consider the cyclical characteristics of credit, credit/GDP. They find that cycles of between 8 and 30 years are more important than those of shorter periodicities in characterising the variables' behaviour. In keeping with other authors, the cycles are possibly twice as long post-1985 compared with before. From Table 6.2, the shift in the peak in GDP's power spectrum supports a lengthening of the key cycle, but not doubling of the periodicity.

Peersman and Pozzi (2007) posit that households with deteriorating balance sheets are more likely to resort to using external finance during a recession. Unsecured lending is relatively high risk so relatively expensive. As incomes rise, unsecured lending should decline: as house prices rise and equity is enhanced, there should be a shift from unsecured to secured. In Table 6.6, unsecured lending has a 10-year peak whilst secured has a 7½-year cycle. Unsecured lending, unsurprisingly, has a higher level of volatility and a higher level of coherence with GDP. Cohesion indicates the linkage is positive, suggesting pro-cyclical rather than counter-cyclical lending. Sync indicates that secured lending, by contrast, is out of phase but not closely related to income. This could reflect the value of equity the repeat buyer may have falling in a recession forcing them to borrow more. Alternatively, a source of wealth to tap to smooth consumption via secured lending is mortgage equity release. Muellbauer (2007) argues that it is housing equity withdrawal proffers the pro-cyclical impact of house prices, rather than a wealth effect. Here, out of phase effects are found which are more consistent with Peersman and Pozzi's deteriorating balance sheet but not quite in the sense they expressed.

GDP leads unsecured but follows secured lending so both Meen and Chen et al.'s positions on credit and the business cycle are supported. As assessed by the power spectra, the both forms of lending are more volatile than GDP.

6.5.2 Lending and House Prices

Lending and house prices are explored in Table 6.7. Secured lending precedes house prices over the longer cycles. As with GDP, Sync indicates that secured lending is not in phase. This goes against the case of a pro-cyclical impact of house prices on lending, upon which the financial accelerator is based and Aoki et al. (2004) observation that the amount of secured borrowing to finance consumption is closely related to this collateral position. However, housing equity withdrawal or remortgaging is consistent with Peersman and Pozzi's deteriorating balance sheet thesis. That said, both forces could offset each other leading to the low

Table 6.6 Spectral characteristics, short series lending and GDP

Cycle	Power spectrum		Phase	Adjusted gain		Coherence		Co-Spectrum	Coh	Sync
	SEC	GDP	Qtrs	SEC to GDP	GDP to SEC	Coh^2	Sync^2			
10	0.0231	0.010	−6.994	0.531	0.358	0.039	0.151	0.003	0.198	−0.388
7.5	**0.0249**	**0.013**	−9.719	0.671	0.376	0.051	0.202	−0.004	−0.225	−0.449
6	0.0242	0.012	−6.626	0.814	0.506	0.011	0.401	−0.002	−0.105	−0.633
5	0.0158	0.006	−7.428	0.416	0.340	0.068	0.074	−0.002	−0.260	−0.272
4.29	0.0152	0.003	−2.016	0.670	0.943	0.345	0.287	0.004	0.588	−0.535
	UNSEC			UNSEC to GDP	GDP to UNSEC					
10	**0.0743**	0.010	−0.370	0.667	0.837	0.557	0.002	0.020	0.746	−0.043
7.5	0.0644	**0.013**	2.119	0.808	0.678	0.447	0.101	0.019	0.669	0.318
6	0.0365	0.012	0.986	1.013	0.549	0.520	0.036	0.015	0.721	0.190
5	0.0251	0.006	2.891	0.625	0.469	0.111	0.182	0.004	0.333	0.427
4.29	0.0114	0.003	−4.163	0.974	0.597	0.001	0.580	0.000	0.034	−0.762

Bold highlights greatest values
Upper section Secured lending, *lower section* Unsecured lending

Table 6.7 Spectral characteristics, short series lending and HP

Cycle	Power spectrum		Phase	Adjusted gain		Coherence		Co-Spectrum	Coh	Sync
	SEC	HP	Qtrs	SEC to HP	HP to SEC	Coh^2	$Sync^2$			
10	0.0231	**0.112**	−0.924	0.640	0.455	0.285	0.006	0.027	0.534	−0.078
7.5	**0.0249**	0.080	−5.152	0.395	0.424	0.037	0.130	0.009	0.193	−0.361
6	0.0242	**0.102**	−3.452	0.273	0.225	0.024	0.038	0.008	0.153	−0.195
5	0.0158	0.076	6.163	0.190	0.137	0.003	0.023	−0.002	−0.058	0.151
4.29	0.0152	**0.087**	0.118	0.466	0.280	0.130	0.000	0.013	0.361	0.016
	UNSEC			UNSEC to HP	HP to UNSEC					
10	**0.0743**	**0.112**	1.374	0.715	0.947	0.646	0.031	0.073	0.804	0.176
7.5	0.0644	0.080	3.213	0.624	1.002	0.382	0.243	0.044	0.618	0.493
6	0.0365	**0.102**	2.958	0.927	0.665	0.315	0.301	0.034	0.561	0.549
5	0.0251	0.076	3.848	0.383	0.252	0.012	0.085	0.005	0.110	0.291
4.29	0.0114	**0.087**	−3.581	0.613	0.161	0.006	0.092	0.003	0.080	−0.303

Bold highlights greatest values
Upper section Secured lending, *lower section* Unsecured lending

coherence between secured lending and house prices, consistent with Goodhart and Hoffman (2008) in that neither broad money nor credit in the 1985–2006 era affects house price inflation. Inconsistent with Chen et al. (2010), unsecured lending has a close association with house prices at the key cycle of 10 years. Here, gain to lending is around 1. As housing leads lending by 1.4 quarters (18 weeks), lending, not based on, but associated with the increase value of dwellings. Again, this may reflect a balance sheet issue: those overstretched when house purchasing seeking additional borrowing. In a Madsen sense, getting over the first few payments may be the plan.

6.6 Consumer Durables—Deferrable Consumption

6.6.1 Consumer Durables and GDP

There is a reconsideration of the income effect with the subdivision of consumption. Consumption expenditures on durables should be procyclical (Gordon 2013). In Table 6.8, at the key 7½-year cycle for both types of consumption expenditure where cohesion is at a maximum, CDs lead GDP by around 10 weeks, much quicker than Leamer's expectation of 4 to 5 quarters. With a gain value around 1, this suggests that consumer durable spending anticipates or precipitates transitory income growth.

At the 10 cycle where coherence and cohesion with NCD are at a maximum, the gain value is above 1. GDP leads NCD by 20 weeks. These indicators are consistent with HHE. Indeed, so similar are the results to suggest that HHE really is a proxy for NCD.

6.6.2 Consumer Durables and House Prices

With the subdivision of consumption, there can also be a reconsideration of the wealth effect of house prices on types of consumption. Table 6.9 shows that cohesion and coherence are greatest for CDs at the 5-year cycle. The 7½-year periodicity power spectra values are similar

Table 6.8 Spectral characteristics, short series GDP and CD/NCD

Cycle	Power spectrum		Phase	Adjusted Gain		Coherence		Co-Spectrum	Coh	Sync
	CD	GDP	Weeks	CD to GDP	GDP to CD	Coh^2	$Sync^2$			
10	0.0264	0.0102	−8.7	0.841	0.440	0.366	0.004	0.010	0.605	−0.064
7.5	**0.0432**	**0.0132**	−9.7	0.905	0.597	0.527	0.013	**0.017**	0.726	−0.115
6	0.0400	0.0115	−18.4	0.703	0.489	0.298	0.045	0.012	0.546	−0.213
5	**0.0425**	0.0057	−23.5	0.625	0.932	**0.414**	**0.168**	0.010	0.644	−0.410
4.29	0.0218	0.0032	−4.3	0.263	0.361	0.094	0.001	0.003	0.306	−0.037
	NCD			NCD to GDP	GDP to NCD					
10	**0.0070**	0.0102	21.3	0.927	1.043	**0.904**	**0.063**	0.008	0.951	0.250
7.5	**0.0070**	**0.0132**	9.6	0.966	0.844	0.797	0.019	**0.009**	0.892	0.138
6	0.0064	0.0115	5.9	0.905	0.815	0.728	0.010	0.007	0.853	0.101
5	0.0014	0.0057	−15.0	1.230	0.507	0.545	0.078	0.002	0.738	−0.280
4.29	0.0022	0.0032	10.6	0.810	0.916	0.678	0.064	0.002	0.824	0.254

Bold highlights greatest values
Upper section Consumer durables, *lower section* Non-consumer durables

Table 6.9 Spectral characteristics, short series HP and CD/NCD

Cycle	Power spectrum		Phase	Adjusted Gain		Coherence		Co-Spectrum	Coh	Sync
	CD	HP	Qtrs	CD to HP	HP to CD	Coh^2	$Sync^2$			
10	0.0264	**0.112**	−0.081	0.826	0.455	0.376	0.000	0.033	0.613	−0.008
7.5	**0.0432**	0.080	0.568	0.532	0.672	0.353	0.005	0.035	0.594	0.071
6	0.0400	**0.102**	−1.127	0.698	0.643	0.411	0.038	0.041	0.641	−0.195
5	**0.0425**	0.076	−1.658	0.748	0.980	**0.552**	**0.182**	**0.042**	0.743	−0.426
4.29	0.0218	**0.087**	−1.042	1.002	0.588	0.507	0.082	0.031	0.712	−0.286
	NCD			NCD to HP	HP to NCD					
10	**0.0070**	**0.112**	4.510	0.814	0.966	0.454	0.333	**0.019**	0.674	0.577
7.5	**0.0070**	0.080	3.386	0.697	1.166	**0.468**	**0.344**	0.016	0.684	0.587
6	0.0064	**0.102**	2.258	0.605	0.722	0.301	0.136	0.014	0.549	0.368
5	0.0014	0.076	−1.376	1.045	0.378	0.326	0.069	0.006	0.571	−0.263
4.29	0.0022	**0.087**	0.270	0.901	0.435	0.388	0.004	0.009	0.623	0.062

Bold highlights greatest values
Upper section Consumer durables, *lower section* Non-consumer durables

to those at the 5-year cycle but with lower cohesion. The phase values indicate that house prices lead CD at the former but follow at the latter. One would expect new durables to be purchased at the same time as households move home. House price is not the best proxy for relocations, but Stein (1995) argues that they are associated. Also, lending for house purchase in the Ponzi era allowed for such purchases to be secured against the house.

At the 10- and 7½-year cycles where cohesion with NCD is at a maximum, the gain value is around/above one. House prices lead NCD by around a year, perhaps enough time to accept house price changes as persistent and so, following a wealth effect hypothesis, precipitating persistent changes in consumption.

Overall, the 7½-year cycle in GDP in the second era does not appear to drive other cycles. Housing and consumption more strongly feature the 10-year. Consumer durables with a 7½-year cycle could lead an upturn in the trade cycle. Major items of purchase other than a house would be secured against that item if purchased with a loan. Non-durables, the main component of consumption, with a longer cycle appear to reflect the smoothing the PIH suggests, with unsecured lending also having that cycle. Lending would be a key feature of the PIH. However, the lending seems to reflect short not long-term plans, not consistent with PIH.

6.7 House Vintages—Are New Dwelling Different?

New and second-hand housing serve the same function but have slightly differing characteristics. New builds will be constructed with the benefit of contemporary techniques and technologies and are likely to come with a warrantee implying that, for a representative property, the price should be higher. Barras and Ferguson (1985) suggest that property vintages will depreciate at approximately the same rate. As such, there should be a stable ranking of prices for a representative house from each vintage.

With a focus on the property, the nature of interaction between RBs in a Stein (1995) analysis, it is proposed that, as it will not contain a windfall embedded in the price, *New* housing has a different effect on market volatility compared with second-hand dwellings that are put up for sale by RBs. New dwellings capture for the builder the capital that would otherwise be transferred from one homeowner to another. In other words, a new property extracts the capital gain that the second-hand property owner would have used to trade-up. As they will reduce the embedded capital gain in the system, the release of new 'houses' and 'flats' should disinflate second-hand price dynamics doubly: an increase in supply will lower price pressures; and the sale of a new property will withdraw equity from the second-hand market, reducing price volatility. The builder may have less discretion about property supply than the RB. They may be able to accelerate work in progress as prices to rise and drip feed in the decline. However, the builder may need the capital to move on to the next project (Stein 1995).

From the above discussion, it is averred that temporal variations in the numbers of FTBs and new properties in the market will be lower than RBs and second-hand dwellings. As both builders and buyers are dependent on bank finance, they are likely to be co-driven by a third factor, credit. Thus, construction expenditure could lead prices without [Granger] causing them.

The power spectra for *Modern*, *Old*, and *New* dwelling prices are displayed in Figs. 6.7 and 6.8. What is evident is that the power or

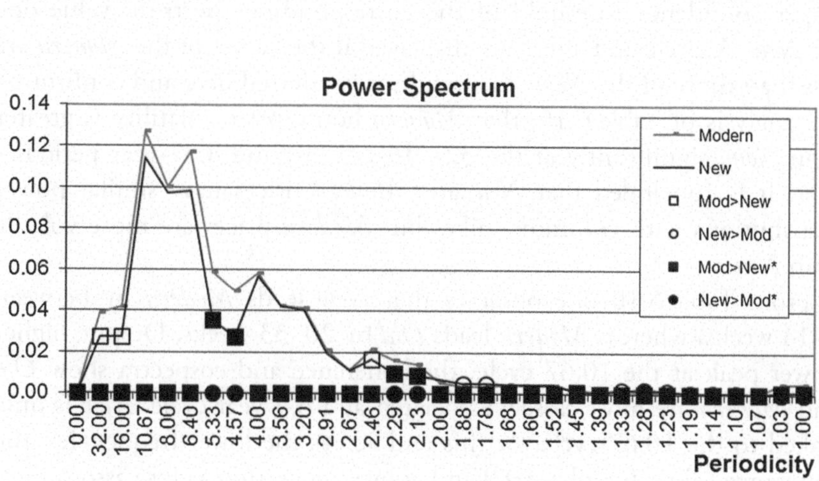

Fig. 6.7 The power spectra for *modern* and *new* house prices

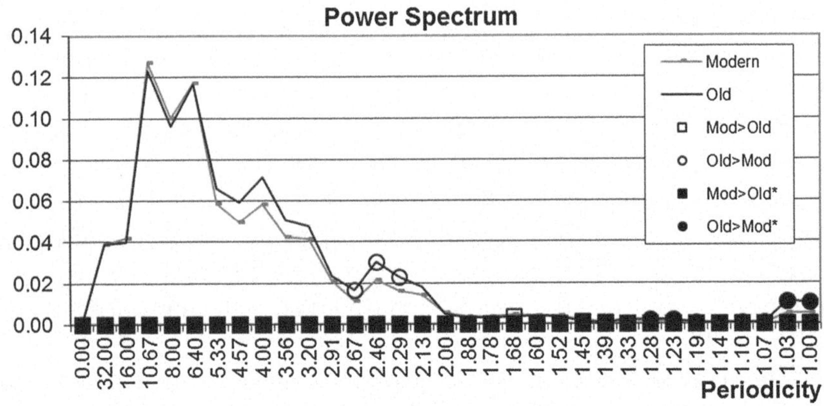

Fig. 6.8 The power spectra for *modern* and *old* house prices

volatility is concentrated at periodicities between 10.67 and 6.4 years. To test the relative volatility hypothesis, a Hughes-Hallett and Richter (2004) test is used. To avoid a plethora of lines on a diagram, the following protocol is adopted. Where a power spectrum *Modern* value is above the 95% upper confidence threshold of the corresponding one for *New* it is signified by a square. A block replaces this if the 95% lower confidence threshold can replace the value and still be above the 95% upper confidence threshold of the corresponding spectrum value one for *New*. A circle and a disc are displayed if the values of the *Modern* are less than those of the *New*. As a result, it is inferred here and confirming the analysis of Table 6.10, that *Modern* house price volatility is greater than *New*, significantly at the 32-, 16-, 5.33-, and 4.57-year periodicities. It is concluded that *New* and *Modern* prices have similar power distributions with common spikes but *Modern* prices are more volatile than *New*'s.

From Table 6.10 one observes that *New* leads *Modern* by between 4–14 weeks, whereas *Modern* leads *Old* by 20–33 weeks. Despite higher power peak at the 10.67 cycle, the coherence and cospectra show *Old* and *Modern* are most closely associated at a 6.4-year cycle. *New* is only linked to the 10.67 cycle. At this and across the lower frequencies, the coherence values for all are 0.9 and above, suggesting a close association, consistent with those among dwelling substitutes.

Table 6.10 Spectral characteristics, vintages

Cycle	Power spectrum		Phase	Adjusted gain		Coherence		Co-Spectrum	Coh	Sync
	New	Mod	Weeks	New to Modern	Modern to New	Coh^2	$Sync^2$			
10.67	0.114	0.127	−3.8	0.954	0.998	0.952	0.000	0.118	0.976	−0.006
8	0.097	0.100	−13.6	0.909	1.034	0.939	0.001	0.095	0.969	−0.028
6.4	0.098	0.117	−13.7	0.958	0.941	0.900	0.001	0.102	0.949	−0.035
	Old	Modern		Old to Modern	Modern to Old					
10.67	0.124	0.127	32.4	1.056	0.934	0.983	0.003	0.124	0.991	0.052
8	0.096	0.100	26.7	1.057	0.927	0.977	0.003	0.097	0.988	0.057
6.4	0.116	0.117	19.6	1.047	0.949	0.991	0.003	0.116	0.996	0.053
	Old	New		Old to New	New to Old					
10.67	0.124	0.114	48.3	1.072	0.906	0.965	0.006	0.117	0.982	0.077
8	0.096	0.097	50.1	1.123	0.866	0.962	0.011	0.095	0.981	0.106
6.4	0.116	0.098	38.8	0.987	0.911	0.889	0.010	0.101	0.943	0.099

As showing in Fig. 6.8, *Modern* and *Old* house price power spectra are almost identical. As posited, *New* house prices have lower power, notably at 5.33- and the 4.57-year cycles. Consistent with the equity extraction thesis, construction expenditure has a corresponding 5-year peak.

Cook and Holly (2000) find non-synchronised, common cycles among the three series. Table 6.10 does not display evidence of this asynchronicity at common cycles.

6.8 Buyer Groups and the Recycling of Dwellings

The power spectra for FTB and RB are displayed in Fig. 6.9. What is evident again is that the power or volatility is concentrated at periodicities between 10.67 and 6.4 years. As a result, it is inferred here and confirming the analysis of Table 6.11, that FTB house price volatility is greater than RB, significantly at the 10.67-year periodicity. It is concluded that FTB and RB prices have similar power distributions with common spikes but the FTB prices are more volatile than RBs', importantly, at the key market cycle for FTB.

Values for the buyer group spectra are displayed in Table 6.11. The peak power spectrum value for the repeat buyer (highlighted in bold)

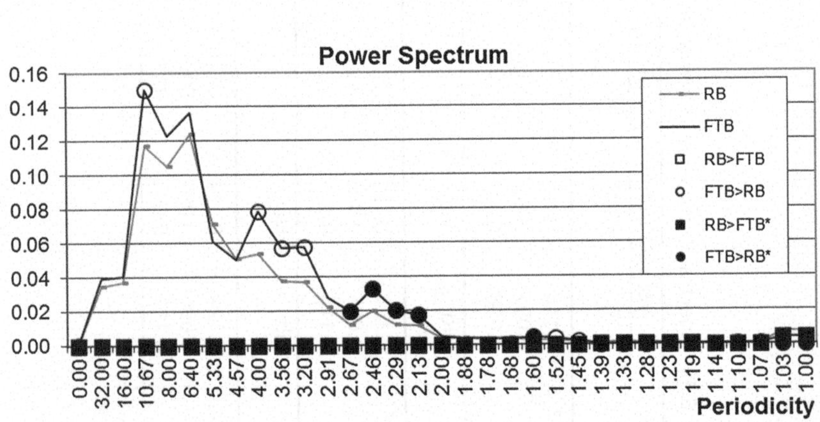

Fig. 6.9 The power spectra for FTB and RB house prices

Table 6.11 Spectral characteristics of buyer groups: by three filters

Cycle	Power spectrum		Phase	Gain		Coherence		Cosp	Coh	Sync
	FTB	RB	Days	FTB to RB	RB to FTB	Coh^2	$Sync^2$			
10.67	**0.150**	0.117	72	0.875	1.122	**0.969**	0.013	**0.130**	0.984	0.115
8	0.123	0.105	76	0.905	1.062	0.936	0.026	0.110	0.967	0.161
6.4	0.137	**0.124**	39	0.922	1.017	0.928	0.011	0.125	0.963	0.103
CF										
10.67	0.217	0.152	110	0.836	1.191	**0.963**	0.031	0.178	0.981	0.177
8	**0.222**	**0.169**	85	0.861	1.132	0.942	0.032	**0.188**	0.971	0.180
6.4	0.197	0.164	61	0.884	1.064	0.915	0.025	0.172	0.957	0.159
BW										
10.67	**0.154**	0.120	72	0.875	1.122	**0.969**	0.013	**0.134**	0.984	0.114
8	0.126	0.107	76	0.905	1.063	0.936	0.026	0.112	0.967	0.160
6.4	0.140	**0.126**	40	0.922	1.019	0.928	0.011	0.128	0.963	0.103

Bold highlights greatest values
Upper section Hodrick-Prescott, *Middle section* Christiano-Fitzgerald, *lower section* Butterworth

occurs at the 6.4-year cycle, whereas the peak value on the power spectrum for first-time buyers is found at the 10.67-year periodicity. In both cases, the value for RB is less than that for FTB. So, not only is the price trend greater but the volatility is also. Smith and Tesarek (1991) found higher volatility for more expensive housing. The RB price volatility is not greater than FTB's at the second-shorter cycle.

The peak cospectrum value, the one that indicates the confluence is greatest, occurs at this 10.67-year cycle. Using the peak of the cospectrum as the benchmark for assessing co-relations, the 10.67-year cycle is the one where the RB and FTB are most confluent.

As reported in Table 6.11, phase converted into time domain values suggests that the repeat buyer market leads the FTB by between 39 and 76 days. These are less than a three-month lag, so difficult to discern using quarterly data with some other techniques. There is evidence that the RB market is the one that responds to shocks earlier or drives changes in the FTB market. Again, not the outcome expected from OMR. Coulson and McMillen (2007) find better lead lesser worse quality house prices. Although not precisely cheap versus expensive or low versus high-quality housing, the FTB would be buying a cheaper dwelling than a repeat buyer. As such, the finding is consistent with Coulson and McMillen (2007).

The link between the FTB and RB house price volatility as posited by OMR is that the former should magnify the latter. The adjusted gain values of 1.122 and 1.017 in Table 6.11 show that, with values, the amplitude of the cycle for the repeat buyer amplifies that of the first-time buyer at the 10.67 and the 6.4-year cycles, which is not what Sommervoll et al. and OMR posited.

6.8.1 Do Alternative Cycle Decompositions Affect Results?

As a key theme concerns cyclicality, Butterworth's (BW) and Christiano-Fitzgerald's (CF) filters are employed to provide some contrast to the H-P results. The settings for the CF are minimum and maximum periodicities of 2 and 40. The BW is set with a maximum value of 40 and MA(2). The Butterworth values are almost identical to the Hodrick Prescott, confirming that the 1600 setting corresponds with 10-year. The CF values provide a slightly different picture. Here, the 8-year is the major cycle common to both buyers. Here, the FTB prices are more volatile whilst they follow RB prices with a lag of 85 days. Overall, the differences between the three filters do not alter any key inferences.

6.9 The Ripple Effect and Buyer Groups

Wood (2003) suggests it is possible that the South East responds more quickly to national economic shocks (consistent with a *shock* perspective), or the South East leads the economic cycle and, hence, is a leading region (consistent with a *cycle* perspective). Given Meen's definition, a ripple entails a series of regional house prices that increase in an order identified by distance from the leading region. An urban system would also see a Southern Eastern leadership. Hierarchy implies regions with the largest cities should respond before others. Yorkshire-Humberside should lead East Midlands with a hierarchy hypothesis but lag with a ripple hypothesis.

The UK as the national series will influence, and be influenced by, regional cycles. If there is a dominant cycle, one would expect it to be featured in London's spectrum. By contrast, regions remote from the leading province should also exhibit the dominant periodicity but also the longest delays. Given overlapping housing markets, one would posit that London (LON), Outer Metropolitan (OMET), and Outer South East (OSE) would all exhibit closely associated power spectra. This will diminish with distance, so that distinctions should be seen to the greatest for Scotland (SC), followed by the North (NO), the North West (NW), Yorkshire-Humberside (YH), Wales (WA), South West (SW), West Midlands (WM), East Midlands (EM), and East Anglia (EA) in that order. Coherence should be relatively high across all regions at that dominant cycle. Distinctive peaks in a regional power spectrum, which are viewed as indicating local market conditions, could reflect less diversified industrial bases (Marchand 1981), peripherality, or distinct markets.

In Table 6.12 the standard deviations of the filtered series are presented. A series of results emerge. First, the volatility of FTB prices is greater than for RB. One exception, the South West, appears is due to a large outlier. Second, the UK's volatilities are towards the bottom of the range consistent perhaps with a 'portfolio' effect where there is a reduction in volatility of a portfolio of assets that a spread across weakly related asset markets. Alternatively, it reflects a balanced economy model

Table 6.12 Standard deviations of the filtered series

REGION	SD	REGION	SD	REGION	SD
EA FTB	0.0707	NW FTB	0.0586	SW FTB	0.0583
EA RB	0.0622	NW RB	0.0560	SW RB	0.0617
EM FTB	0.0642	OMEFTB	0.0583	WA FTB	0.0625
EM RB	0.0587	OMET RB	0.0493	WA RB	0.0593
LON FTB	0.0558	OSE FTB	0.0645	WM FTB	0.0621
LON RB	0.0506	OSE RB	0.0565	WM RB	0.0581
NO FTB	0.0604	SC FTB	0.0462	YH FTB	0.0702
NO RB	0.0591	SC RB	0.0382	YH RB	0.0583
UK FTB	0.0505			UK RB	0.0458

where the asynchronicity inherent in a ripple reduced the volatility in the weighted average of the regions. Third, the leading and highest priced markets have relatively low levels of volatility. London and Outer Metropolitan markets have the lowest English regional volatility. Fourth, those regions adjacent to the Outer South East appear to be the most volatile. This could reflect the volatility one might expect in low areas at the extreme edge of commuting. Fifth, Scotland appears different and indeed has a distinct house auction system. That said, Thanos and White (2014) show auctions can be subject to volatility variations. Sixth, the ranking of FTB and RB volatilities appear similar, which suggests that the same forces are common to FTB and RB across the country.

In Table 6.13 are the peak values of the power spectra are highlighted in bold for both FTBs and RBs. As is evident, the regions generally reflect the national division. Peak volatility occurs are the 10.67-year cycle for the largest minority of regions for FTB, whereas this 6.4-year cycle performs the same function for RBs. In five cases, the FTB and RB are at a peak at a common cycle. As the power spectrum is a

Table 6.13 Regional spectral characteristics

Cycle	FTB			RB			Region
	Coherence	Power	Cospectrum	Coherence	Power	Cospectrum	
	0.923	**0.259**	**0.189**	0.958	0.191	0.146	EM
	0.763	**0.174**	**0.133**	0.756	0.119	**0.093**	LON
10.67	0.708	**0.176**	**0.136**	**0.760**	0.188	**0.119**	NO
	0.879	**0.174**	**0.140**	0.839	**0.104**	**0.095**	OMET
	0.686	0.081	**0.032**	**0.778**	**0.079**	**0.042**	SC
	0.838	**0.235**	**0.170**	0.886	0.186	0.134	WA
	0.678	0.143	0.102	0.691	**0.131**	0.086	LON
	0.508	0.153	0.098	0.544	**0.236**	0.088	NO
8	0.658	**0.252**	0.117	0.797	**0.209**	0.110	NW
	0.460	**0.083**	0.008	0.651	0.077	0.021	SC
	0.875	**0.260**	0.167	0.962	0.206	0.144	WM
	0.836	0.270	0.165	0.704	**0.211**	0.109	YH
	0.939	**0.273**	0.172	0.966	**0.230**	**0.149**	EA
	0.884	0.256	0.176	**0.967**	**0.223**	**0.164**	EM
	0.942	**0.231**	0.156	0.943	**0.200**	**0.142**	OSE
6.4	0.939	**0.193**	0.152	**0.975**	**0.196**	**0.146**	SW
	0.872	0.218	0.157	**0.904**	**0.198**	**0.142**	WA
	0.924	0.260	0.180	**0.979**	**0.235**	**0.168**	WM
	0.867	**0.285**	0.180	**0.823**	0.189	0.125	YH

Bold highlights greatest values

reflection of standard deviation, one would expect the values would highlight the same rankings of volatility. As it turns out, with the exceptions of the North and South West, the values at the peak of the power spectra are correlated with the corresponding standard deviation. The South West has an outlier point, noted above; the North is not easy to explain.

The power spectrum FTB peak at the 10.67-year cycle for the UK is also reflected in those cospectra for EM, OMET, SC, LON, N and WA. Of these, the peak of the power spectra of both FTBs and RBs occurs at that cycle of OMET, but coherence is not at a maximum. SC exhibits a peak in the RBs spectrum, whereas the rest are associated with FTBs cycle. From the national and regional evidence, the 10.67-year periodicity is more closely associated with the FTB.

There is a confluence of FTB and RB peaks for SW, EA and OSE at the 6.4-year cycle. The power spectrum for the RB for the UK, EM, and WM and that of the FTB for YH also are associated with the 6.4-year cycle. This shorter cycle combines regions surrounding the south east. In a sense, this is the housing market reach or shadow of London.

6.9.1 Is Price Diffusions Better Explained by Urban Systems Theory?

One could posit that the ripple effect should be evident in both FTB and RB data. The results in Table 6.14 involve the region–nation pairwise relationship discussed in Chap. 4. Converting the phase value into the time domain, the delay reported corresponds to the highest power spectrum value. For example, the leading region relative to the benchmark reference cycle is found to be London, which leads the UK series at the 8-year cycle by 2.54 quarters. At the other end of the spectrum, Scotland lags the UK by 7.2 quarters, at the 10.67-year cycle.

There is evidence for the ripple effect in repeat buyers. The southern lead (negative sign on phase) the reference cycle and the northern regions lag the UK. Within the southern grouping, the order is imperfect in that the Outer South East lags East Anglia. The northern regions are in an appropriate order for the ripple.

Table 6.14 Ripple effect: RB in quarters

	Cycle	Phase	Power	Coh	Sync
LON	8	−2.546	0.131	0.729	−0.398
OMET	10.67	−2.417	0.104	0.858	−0.319
EA	6.4	−1.847	0.230	0.884	−0.430
OSE	6.4	−1.533	0.200	0.903	−0.357
SW	6.4	−1.290	0.196	0.938	−0.307
EM	6.4	−0.051	0.223	0.983	−0.012
WM	6.4	0.290	0.235	0.987	0.070
WA	6.4	1.193	0.198	0.910	0.275
YH	8	2.587	0.211	0.733	0.408
NW	8	2.971	0.209	0.745	0.492
NO	8	3.587	0.236	0.562	0.478
SC	10.67	7.165	0.079	0.435	0.768

For the hierarchy thesis, the core city-regions should be more closely linked to the reference cycle. Cohesion values in Table 6.14 follow inverted *U*-shaped. In other words, the Midlands regions are more closely associated with the UK. The low level of cohesion is not predicted where London is the dominant, integrated market. The measure of synchronicity is similar to the phase ordering. Also, the highest power spectrum value occurs at the 6.4-year cycle for the Midlands regions.

The delays in ripple effect in RBs should be reflected in FTBs. In Table 6.15, again the London and the south east lead and the northern regions lag the reference FTB UK house prices. There is a general link between distance and asynchronicity consistent with a ripple effect. However, the order is not the same as with RBs. The London area still leads, but the actual leader region is Outer Metropolitan. Despite this switching, the contiguity is still good. The ripple can be seen to spread from the leader through Outer South East to East Anglia, the South West and the East Midlands.

Cohesion appears elevated relative to RBs and the response delays are lengthier, suggesting it takes longer for price changes to pass across space and that regions are more attuned to the nation. It could be that prices diffuse between buyers and regions via the RB. The RB acts as a marker locally and when searching in a neighbouring region.

The North stands out as a ripple anomaly. FTBs respond possibly three quarters too early and have a very low level of volatility. Other regions are broadly in line with the RB order. Indeed, the timings also are similar.

Table 6.15 Ripple effect: FTB in quarters

	Cycle	Phase	Power	Coh	Sync
OMET	10.67	−2.703	0.174	0.864	−0.363
LON	10.67	−2.375	0.174	0.820	−0.299
OSE	6.4	−1.790	0.231	0.878	−0.413
EA	6.4	−1.672	0.273	0.889	−0.387
SW	6.4	−1.046	0.193	0.937	−0.246
EM	10.67	−0.507	0.259	0.958	−0.072
NO	10.67	0.351	0.176	0.841	0.044
WM	8	0.382	0.260	0.933	0.070
YH	6.4	0.818	0.285	0.913	0.186
WA	10.67	1.158	0.235	0.902	0.155
NW	8	3.092	0.252	0.666	0.463
SC	8	7.376	0.083	0.083	0.673

6.10 Time Domain Confirmation—Unit Root Tests

The spectral methods here analyse the cyclical element from a series decomposition. To consider the trend, there is an application of non-stationary methods; specifically unit root tests. Sommervoll et al. and OMR imply that, in the long-run, the differential tends towards equilibrium. The former implies a common cyclical pattern whereas the latter posits a long term stable RB FTBs ratio.

An examination of unit root is undertaken using a variety of methods. In Table 6.16, the results from three methods on individual expressions are reported for each region by buyer group with intercept and trend. The ADF results indicate that all the series are non-stationary. This is confirmed by the ADF tests due Park and Fuller, and the KPSS tests.

Following Pesaran (2007a, b), there is a consideration of a pairwise differential relationship. The first examination is of the RB: FTB ratio. The three tests (KPSS, 1.6163; ADF-PF(1) −1.0488; ADF(1) −0.66133) suggest that it is non-stationary, which is consistent with the data in Tables 5.3 and 5.4 where FTB growth is greater than RB over the 32 years. As such, one can reconsider the leadership of RB over FTB found with spectral analysis using the buyer group prices in differences.

Table 6.16 Unit root tests FTB and RB

	FTB			RB		
	KPSS	ADF–PF	ADF	KPSS	ADF-PF	ADF
NO	0.24884	(3) −2.0347	(3) −1.6997	0.16778	(4) −2.3110	(4) −2.0374
YH	0.17405	(3) −2.4791	(3) −2.2650	0.15930	(4) −2.5599	(4) −2.3804
NW	0.17112	(3) −2.1999	(3) −2.0091	0.16386	(3) −2.5259	(3) −2.3256
EM	0.16571	(3) −2.1969	(3) −2.1242	0.17189	(3) −2.3411	(3) −2.2055
WM	0.17487	(4) −2.8000	(4) −2.6740	0.16966	(4) −2.7568	(4) −2.6595
EA	0.17437	(3) −2.4743	(3) −2.2923	0.18107	(8) −2.9874	(8) −2.7649
OSE	0.21480	(2) −2.2846	(2) −2.0324	0.18977	(9) −1.9490	(9) −2.5154
OMET	0.20180	(2) −2.2829	(2) −2.0918	0.17892	(4) −2.5124	(4) −2.4906
LON	0.22200	(4) −2.7540	(4) −2.5211	0.19006	(3) −2.3174	(3) −2.2758
SW	0.20624	(4) −2.4904	(4) −2.2379	0.18252	(5) −2.3426	(5) −3.0849
WA	0.18106	(3) −2.1505	(3) −1.8661	0.17799	(4) −2.5173	(4) −2.2285
SC	0.17728	(2) −1.9856	(2) −1.6641	0.17736	(4) −2.3376	(4) −0.85847
UK	0.21224	(8) −3.0715	(8) −2.7618	0.18731	(5) −1.9896	(5) −1.8178
CV	0.14847	−3.3947	−3.5101	0.14847	−3.3947	−3.5101

The KPSS tests utilises a kernel of 4, which is approximately $0.75T^{1/3}$. The ADF lags are selected using the AIC and are indicated by the values in parentheses. Indicative critical values for the tests are presented (CV)

What is found, using a VAR (9) is that, rather than RB leadership, there is feedback. RB Granger-cause FTB prices ($\chi^2(9) = 43.99[0.000]$) and FTB Granger-cause RB prices $\chi^2(9) = 19.22[0.023]$). This supports the spectral result that RBs lead but could also reflect a circuit of finance from FTB up the housing ladder and through, say, parental support back to FTBs. Goodhart and Hoffman (2008) reveal RB prices leading FTB.

Holmes (2007) and Holmes and Grimes (2008) use region–nation differentials to establish convergence to the UK reference series. Convergence in this context implies the regions will maintain a stable relationship with the reference cycle in the long run but with deviations in the short. The finding of multi-regional cointegration is consistent with a ripple effect. However, Carvalho and Harvey (2005) argue that if one region is diverging, this will affect the reference national average, undermining the method.

The approach here mirrors the spectral analysis and Holmes and Grimes (2008) as also using region–nation approach, but with the additionally of having two results for each region FTB and RB. Constructing the differential of the region over the nation, Table 6.17 reports the KPSS, ADF and ADF test due to Park and Fuller unit root tests, presuming no trend in the differential. A [positive] trend would imply RB house prices persistently dislocating from FTB.

The differential is shown to be stationary for FTB in the North West, Wales and Scotland, whereas with RB cases are Outer Metropolitan, Yorkshire/Humberside, Outer South East and South West. Non-stationary differentials are concentrated around Outer South East. Agreement among the three sets of tests is not notable, and the same can be said for the regions.

Using the lags highlighted in Table 6.17 for the ADF test, a CD statistic of −0.061 [0.95] and 0.924 [0.355] for the RBs' and FTBs' residuals, respectively, indicates that there is cross-sectional independence among the regional markets. For completeness, the last stage in the pairwise analysis involves the CADF statistic. Only one case of convergence is revealed with CADF and a minority with others unit root tests. Convergence is not common. Carvalho and Harvey's point may be salient. If London is diverging from the rest, this will affect the reference national average, undermining the method. Montagnoli and Nagayasu (2015) arguments rather than their (trend) results imply that London has distinctive cycles, possibly as a result of it being linked into a global financial system (Fernandez et al. 2016; Holly et al. 2011). Abbott and De Vita (2012) find convergence *within* Greater London is incomplete. Notably, they find a City of London cluster, which would correspond well with the safe haven thesis, intimating that mobile capital is distorting the central London housing market. As convergence among London boroughs is not found, and with London growing 50% more quickly than most other regions, convergence for all regions is unlikely. Holmes and Grimes (2008) may have a case in saying there is convergence among regional house prices to the UK average in the pre-2008 era. The post-crisis period is likely to be different.

Next, there is a consideration of vintages. Here, again inferences from spectral work can be reviewed. Table 6.18 contains the unit root tests for both the three series in levels (with trend) and then in

Table 6.17 Pairwise unit root tests

	FTB				RB			
	KPSS	ADF-PF	ADF	CADF	KPSS	ADF-PF	ADF	CADF
NO	1.9917	(1) 0.49369	(1) −1.9989	−2.2755	0.45364	(2) −2.0705	(2) −2.1295	−2.6901
YH	1.1068	(4) −1.6801	(4) −1.5319	−2.2186	**0.17649**	**(4) −2.6754**	(4) −2.4081	−2.2527
NW	**0.39437**	(3) −0.81845	(3) −2.2612	−2.8759	0.63812	**(3) −2.6725**	(3) −2.6071	−3.0103
EM	0.50320	(1) 0.66067	(1) −2.1888	−2.4319	1.6255	(1) −1.4820	(1) −1.5126	−0.25942
WM	0.56282	(1) 0.59137	(4) −1.9671	−2.1877	1.2639	(1) −1.1818	(1) −0.86191	−0.72699
EA	0.96230	(5) −2.0693	(5) −2.2940	−2.8461	1.1048	(2) −2.4972	(2) −2.2809	−1.6208
OSE	0.83780	(4) −0.23700	(4) −2.6437	−2.5662	**0.30923**	**(6) −2.6507**	(6) −2.3614	−1.9009
OMET	0.98864	(4) −0.17908	(4) −2.3897	−2.0146	**0.34337**	**(3) −3.2026**	**(3) −2.9837**	−2.9475
LON	**0.35363**	(5) −1.0358	(5) −2.5041	−2.5262	0.82360	(2) −1.5874	(3) −1.7431	−1.7055
SW	1.2273	(1) −0.51892	(1) −2.1977	−2.1575	**0.12681**	**(2) −3.3409**	**(2) −4.9819**	−2.6894
WA	**0.19771**	(5) −1.4207	(4) −2.2354	−2.3930	0.77198	(4) −2.1424	(4) −2.4992	−3.0530
SC	**0.39796**	(5) −2.1963	(5) −2.6826	−2.9864	0.64086	**(6) −3.0006**	**(6) −3.3142**	**−3.4236**
CV	0.44403	−2.5454	−2.8217	−3.25	0.44403	−2.5454	−2.8217	−3.25

Table 6.18 Unit root tests vintages

	KPSS	ADF-PF	ADF
New	0.19510	(6) −2.4362	(6) −2.2105
Old	0.19912	(8) −3.0955	(8) −2.8623
Mod	0.19510	(7) −2.6002	(7) −2.6325
CV	0.14847	−3.3947	−3.5101
New−Mod	1.8020	(4) −1.3473	(4) −2.0530
New−Old	2.5285	(7) 0.40491	(7) −0.94682
Mod–Old	2.4991	(7) 1.0525	(7) 0.69436
CV	0.44403	−2.5454	−2.8217

Bold highlights those cases of finding stationarity (at the 5% level)

Table 6.19 Granger causality tests vintages

To / From	New	Old	Modern
New		(6) .149	(6) .473
Old	(6) .000		(5) .111
Modern	(6) .000	(5) .000	

p-values
Number in the bracket is the lag order

ratio form. What is found is that there are no cases of stationary data being revealed. There appears to be a change in structure. The data in Table 5.5 indicates that *New* dwellings grew slowly. At a time of high house prices, a shift towards smaller dwellings would be likely. As such, a general change in the relative costs would be likely.

The spectral work indicated that at the key cycles *Modern* leads *Old* and both follow *New*. Given there is no long-term relationship between the three series, Granger-causality is considered in Table 6.19. Using a VAR (6) and (5) respectively, *Modern* Granger causes both *New* and *Old*: *Old* causes *New* suggesting *New* follows rather than leads the other two. This is at odds with the Spectral work. However, both spectral analysis and Granger-causality find *Modern* leading *Older* dwelling prices, in the case of the former by 20 weeks. The leadership of *New* is empirical rather than a theoretical question. Stein's notion of 'fishing', setting a high price out of line with current market conditions, corresponds with speculative building in expectation of future heightened demand. But if quick sales are required to fund the next project, the going rate set by *Modern* could be the marker. The Spectral results are at longer cycles only. Granger-causality could pick up shorter-term forces ignored by the above analysis.

6.11 What Is Inferred from the Results?

6.11.1 A Persistent Cyclical Perspective of the Ripple Effect

It was proposed that, a ripple in a cycle perspective requires common regional cycles. This is consistent with Sommervoll et al.'s model. Three cycles dominate both buyer groups. However, the Midlands regions more strongly feature shorter cycles, which is more related to repeat buyers.

A second proposal was that regional cyclical agreement declines as the delay between London and the other region is extended. This is not supported. Rather the coherence values are highest with the Midlands regions. This is consistent with a ripple/balanced economy rather that an urban systems model of house price diffusion.

6.11.2 Price Leadership and Overlapping Markets

The implication of comments on Sommervoll et al. (2010: 565) that flat prices leading changes in RB through the provision of equity is problematic. OMR also predicts FTB leadership. Volatility, as assessed by standard deviation and by the power spectra, indicates that FTB prices are more volatile than RBs' in most regions. Fluctuations in the FTB market are not amplified in the RB market.

Finding that RB price lead [and follow] FTB prices is consistent with other 'ripple' work that points to more expensive house prices leading less expensive (Coulson and McMillen 2007; Ho et al. 2008; Hui 2011; Smith and Ho 1996). Turning to the explanations adapted from spatial diffusion literature that predict a top-down transfer one could suggest first, prices are driven by expectations. It could be that the more expensive repeat buyer dwelling acts as a marker, signalling changes in cheaper properties around 11 weeks later. Combine this with adaptive expectation of nominal prices with spillover from neighbouring areas (McDonald 1985), there is a potential mechanism for interlinked, persistent regional cycles.

Second, for conceptualisation purposes, quality tiers are presumed to be overlapping. As sub-market prices become less affordable in more expensive markets, repeat buyers may be forced to search in lower quality tiers of the market, affecting those that would appeal to FTBs. Third, both FTB and RB are subject to banks' credit policies and mortgage rates. A relaxation of credit restrictions does not seem to favour consumption or investment finance; banks are equally incapable of assessing repayment capacity (Schularick and Taylor 2012). As such, the two buyer groups would exhibit similar dynamics, but the RB is better placed to arrange finance. Fourth, when the differential is suitably large, trading down from a more expensive/larger to a smaller/cheaper abode, possibly in a different region, is a further avenue for expensive driving cheaper dwellings.

The spectral results are in accord with Goodhart and Hoffman (2008) revealing RB prices leading FTB. Drawing from an expectations view, it could be that the more expensive repeat buyer dwelling acts as a marker, signalling changes in cheaper properties, which respond around 11 weeks later. This could reflect changes in funding policy by lenders or a shifting of search activity to cheaper markets, possibly in differing regions.

References

Abbott, A., & De Vita, G. (2012). Pairwise Convergence of District-level House Prices in London, *Urban Studies, 49,* 721–741.

Aikman, D., Haldane, A., & Nelson, B. (2014). Curbing the credit cycle. *The Economic Journal, 125,* 1072–1109.

Aoki, K., Proudmand, J., & Vlieghe, G. (2004). House Prices, Consumption and Monetary Policy: a Financial Accelerator Approach, *Journal of Financial Intermediation, 13,* 414–435.

Attanasio, O., Leicester, A., & Wakefield, M. (2011). Do house prices drive consumption growth? The coincident cycles of house prices and consumption in the UK. *Journal of the European Economic Association, 9*(3), 399–435.
Barker, K. (2003). *Review of Housing supply: Interim report—Analysis*. London: HMSO.
Barras, R., & Ferguson, D. (1985). A spectral analysis of building cycles in Britain. *Environment and Planning A, 17*, 1369–1391.
Calderon, C., & Fuentes, J. (2014). Have business cycle changed over the last two decades? An empirical investigation. *Journal of Development Studies, 109*, 98–123.
Campbell, J., & Mankiw, N. G. (1991). The response of consumption to income: A cross-country investigation. *European Economic Review, 35*(4), 723–756.
Carvalho, V., & Harvey, A. (2005). Growth, cycles and convergence in US regional time series. *International Journal of Forecasting, 21*, 667–686.
Chen, M.-C., Kawaguchi, Y., & Patel, K. (2004). An analysis of the trends and cyclical behaviours of house prices in the Asian markets. *Journal of Property Investment & Finance, 22*(1), 55–75.
Chen, N.-K., Chen, S.-S., & Chou, Y.-H. (2010). House prices, collateral constraints, and the asymmetric effect on consumption. *Journal of Housing Economics, 19*, 26–37.
Cook, S., & Holly, S. (2000). Statistical properties of UK house prices: An analysis of disaggregated vintages. *Urban Studies, 37*, 2045–2051.
Coulson, N., & McMillen, D. (2007). The dynamics of intraurban quantile house price indexes. *Urban Studies, 44*(8), 1517–1537.
Dicks, M. (1989). The Housing Market, *Bank of England Quarterly Bulletin*, February, 66–75.
Drehmann, M., Borio, C., & Tstasaronis, K. (2012, June). *Characterising the financial cycle: Don't lose sight of the medium term!* (BIS Working Papers No. 380), Bank for International Settlements.
Fernandez, R., Hofman, A. & Albers, M. (2016). London and New York as a Safe Deposit Box for the Transnational Wealth Elite, *Environment and Planning A, 48*(12), 2443–2461.
Goodhart, C., & Hofmann, B. (2008). House prices, money, credit, and the macroeconomy. *Oxford Review of Economic Policy, 24*(1), 180–205.
Gordon, R. (2013). *Macroeconomics* (12th ed.). New Yok: Prentice Hall.
Ho, L., Ma, Y., & Haurin, D. (2008). House price changes across quality tiers. *Journal of Real Estate Finance & Economics, 37*(4), 299–316.

Holly, S., Pesaran, H., & Yamagata, T. (2011). The Spatio-Temporal Diffusion of House Prices in the UK, *Journal of Urban Economics, 69*(1), 2–23.

Holmes, M. (2007). How convergent are regional house prices in the United Kingdom? Some new evidence from panel data unit root testing. *Journal of Economic and Social Research, 9*(1), 1–17.

Holmes, M., & Grimes, A. (2008). Is there long-run convergence among regional house prices in the UK? *Urban Studies, 45*(8), 1531–1544.

Hoover, K. (2012). *Applied intermediate macroeconomics*. New York: CUP.

Hughes-Hallett, A., & Richter, C. (2004). Spectral analysis as a tool for financial policy: An analysis of the short-end of the British term structure. *Computational Economics, 23,* 271–288.

Hui, H.-C. (2011). Cycles in landed and non-landed housing sub-markets in Malaysia. *International Journal of Housing Markets and Analysis, 4*(2), 144–154.

Levy, D., & Dezhbakhshb, H. (2003). International evidence on output fluctuation and shock persistence. *Journal of Monetary Economics, 50,* 1499–1530.

Madsen, J. (2012). A behavioural model of house prices. *Journal of Economics Behaviour & Organisation, 82,* 21–38.

Marchand, C. (1981). Maximum entropy spectra and the spatial and temporal dimensions of economic fluctuations in an urban system. *Geographical Analysis, 13,* 95–116.

McDonald, J. (1985). Expectations and urban housing prices. *Urban Studies, 22,* 543–549.

Meen, G. (2000). Housing cycles and efficiency. *Scottish Journal of Political Economy, 47*(2), 114–140.

Muellbauer, J. (2007). Housing, credit and consumer expenditure. In *Proceedings-Economic Policy Symposium-Jackson Hole* (pp. 267–334), Federal Reserve Bank of Kansas City.

Peersman, G., & Pozzi, L. (2007, November). *Business cycle fluctuations and excess sensitivity of private consumption* (Bank of England Working Paper No. 335).

Pesaran, M. H. (2007a). A pair-wise approach to testing for output and growth convergence. *Journal of Econometrics, 138,* 312–355.

Pesaran, M. H. (2007b). A simple panel unit root test in the presence of cross-section dependence. *Journal of Applied Econometrics, 22,* 265–312.

Schularick, M., & Taylor, A. (2012). Credit booms gone bust: Monetary policy, leverage cycles, and financial crises, 1870–2008. *American Economic Review, 102*(2), 1029–1061.

Sheiner, L. (1995). Housing prices and the savings of renters. *Journal of Urban Economics, 38*(1), 94–125.

Smith, K. (2001). Pre- and Post-1987 crash frequency domain analysis among pacific rim equity markets. *Journal of Multinational Financial Management, 11*(1), 69–87.

Smith, L., & Ho, M. (1996). The relative price differential between higher and lower priced homes. *Journal of Housing Economics, 5,* 1–17.

Smith, B., & Tesarek, W. (1991). House Prices and regional real estate cycles: Market adjustments in Houston. *Real Estate Economics, 19*(3), 396–416.

Sommervoll, D., Borgersen, T.-A., & Wennemo, T. (2010). Endogenous housing market cycles. *Journal of Banking & Finance, 34*(3), 557–567.

Stein, J. (1995). Prices and trading volume in the housing market: A model with downpayment effects. *The Quarterly Journal of Economics, 110,* 379–405.

Thanos, S., & White, M. (2014). Expectation adjustment in the housing market: Insights from the auction system in Scotland. *Housing Studies, 29*(3), 339–361.

Wood, R. (2003). The information of regional house prices: Can they be used to improve national house price forecasts? *Bank of England Quarterly Bulletin, 43*(3), 304–314.

7

Contributions to the Field and Policy Implications

Abstract This chapter reviews what we have learned about housing cycles. The filtered work is undertaken in nominal terms. Work using real data will have to contend with combination of cycles from both the nominal series and the deflator series, which could generate spurious measures of co-movement. The spectral work indicates that there is evidence of the 'great moderation' in Price, Construction Expenditure, Income, and Consumption within longer cycles in the post 1984 era. Secured lending is not closely related to income or house prices, supporting Goodhart and Hoffman in that that neither broad money nor credit in the 1985–2006 era affect house price inflation. Unsecured lending, by contrast, is. Indeed, it implies that the wealth effect may be expressed through unsecured lending.

It is concluded that as London appears to decouple from the rest over the 32 years, there is some but not general convergence. Against expectations, it is found that repeat buyer house prices act as a marker for first-time buyers. This interpretation is transposed to types of dwelling as well as to regions. The general view is that there is price leadership from more to less expensive housing.

It is suggested that further research is needed in the areas of intergenerational transfers and the role of the buy-to-let purchaser who crowds

D. Gray, *Cycles in the UK Housing Economy*,
DOI 10.1007/978-3-319-63348-0_7

out the first-time buyer, leading to potential social exclusion as dwellings become less affordable for those without rich family members.

Keywords House prices · House buyers · Housing economy · UK housing · House market

This work examines the interaction between UK and regional house price cycles and associated macroeconomics variables, using, in the main, spectral analysis. There has been a broad analysis of house prices in the following dimensions: the type of buyer; the vintage of the dwellings; and the region in which the dwelling is located. Prices are considered in conjunction with other variables. These are income, consumer durables and non-durables, secured and unsecured lending, and construction.

A key theme is the cyclical nature of economics variables, particularly long cycles. Although property prices are cyclical in nature, as De Groot and Franses (2008) note, this is not held to be the dominant view in much of the work in this area. Leamer (2007, 2015) argues that housing cycles are business cycles. This is, in part, related to the role of construction expenditure. The investment element is accompanied by other expenditures when houses are purchased, such as durables, and construction jobs. Sommervoll et al. (2010), using some assumptions about the buyers and sellers, their motivations over property ownership as both a consumption and an investment good, and their recognition of the market and financial constraints, simulate cyclical price series. Using spectral analysis, cycles are found to be evident in buyer activity in the manner predicted. More work is needed here to generate a more comprehensive account. A promising avenue for research is the impact of a periodicity in credit which would drive or accommodate prices. Despite its power in predicting crises, cyclical model of credit such as Minsky's is not that detailed and needs a more thorough analysis before housing can build upon it. Leamer's model is the best example perhaps that reflects the descriptive nature of the field as it is.

7.1 Spectral Methods

In this work, it is assumed that variables that are closely associated have common dominant cycle(s) at which one can discern the degree of phase synchronicity. Two adaptations are made to standard spectral measures. First, to place them in common units, the gain values are adjusted by the standard deviation of both series. As a result, the adjusted gain value is interpreted as the impact of a change of one standard deviation in one variable is translated into standard deviations of the other. Amplification implies that gain is greater than one. This is equivalent to a beta value in SPSS regression outputs.

7.2 Length of Series and Cycles

Much of the empirical work revolves around filtered data. The workhorse for quarterly work is the Hodrick-Prescott filter with a setting of 1600. Criticisms from Guay and St-Amant (2005) and Cogley and Nason (1995) suggest that the Hodrick-Prescott filter can inject distortions in the cyclical series. Phillips and Jin (2015) explain the injection, proposing that the smoothing parameter should grow in relation to the sample size to address spurious cycles. Although users commonly see the setting for seasonal data, Harvey and Trimbur (2008) conclude that the H-P filter setting of 1600 value acts as a 9.92-year high-pass filter with that value. A Butterworth filter set for cycles of 10 years generates cycle values that are almost identical to the Hodrick-Prescott, confirming that the 1600 setting corresponds with 10 years. Christiano-Fitzgerald's filter provides slightly different values and peaks. However, the emphasis on three cycles as characterising house prices is not challenged.

So as to capture the influence of Aikman et al. (2014) 13⅓-year periodicity in credit and to address the Phillips and Jin (2015) recommendation, the 60 years' worth of quarterly data is detrended using a 13-year parameter setting. A higher setting, such as Agnello and Schuknecht's 10,000 (15.7 years), would allocate more of the longer cycles to the cyclical element. What emerges is a more volatile cyclical component but with the same notable turning points. For the power spectrum, there is a greater emphasis on the longer cycles. However, with long 60-year series the 10 year cycles appear common, with household expenditure the only series with an emphasis on the medium, 15-year cycle. Although there was some mixed evidence, the longer cycles were not so influential, possibly because of current income constraint placed on demand for goods and services for many over much of the period. Consumption has a longer cycle than income as households have an urge to plan over the cycle. The prospect that cycle may have lengthened is discussed in Sect. 7.3.

A further insight concerns the nature of the detrended data. It shows a stable range of amplitudes over the longer term: cycles do not seem to become move violent over time. Over the 60 years, deflating house prices nominal series by an inflation index, such as a GDP deflator, lowers the slope, but distorts the cycle so that it can be inflated. The real house price cycle in logarithms is the nominal cycle minus the deflator. The cyclical element of inflation is found to be out of synchronisation with house prices, increasing the volatility of the real. Furthermore, it injects cycles not associated with nominal house prices into real house price series. In the frequency domain, two deflated series could have a high cospectrum value related to inflation only. By implication, correlation values would also be affected.

7.3 Changing Cycles

De Groot and Franses (2008) argue that the system robustness is based on stable cycles. What is found in house prices, consumption, income, and construction is that, in the era of the great moderation (1985–2007), there was a greater emphasis on longer cycles. One could conclude that cycles are not robust. Alternatively, the consumption horizon may have lengthened and amplitude is lower suggesting smoothing over a longer period. This could be related to, in a less credit-constrained era, consumption that is free(r) to move towards that level associated with permanent income (Campbell and Mankiw 1991). Cycles in consumption reflect those in income but with lower volatility, consistent with the

PIH. That said, counter to Cutler (1995), the financially liberal era does not appear to have changed the intensification of the link between consumption and income.

At a 5.45-year cycle, there is a negative relationship between house prices and consumption. Muellbauer (2007) posits that there is an aggregate consumption effect due to the down payment a FTB must make implying as prices rise consumption may fall in unsophisticated credit markets. There is some evidence of this 'first-time buyer sacrifice' in the 60-year period, but it is not there in the second half, consistent with Muellbauer and the liberalisation of mortgage finance in that second period.

Attanasio et al. (2011) note that, over the 40 years from the early 1970s, large increases in house prices were mirrored by consumption booms. There are symptoms of a strong wealth effect in the second era, which not there in the first era.

Over the short-run, it is suggested that construction responds to price signals, whereas the reverse is the case in the long, suggesting the supply has an influence in the long but not over a short horizon. However, the increasing price elasticity of supply with a longer horizon is not so evident in the second era. If supply places less downwards force on prices in a Minskyan world, it could herald an era of a larger bubble: in Leamer's world, the housing cycles would be longer.

7.4 House Prices and Consumption at the National Level

Aikman et al. (2014) suggest that variations in GDP do not account much for perturbations in credit, and that UK loans or credit provision is pro-cyclical, with amplitude twice that of the general business cycle, as proxied by real GDP, but a periodicity that is twice as long as the one for GDP. What is found here is a pro-cyclical 10-year cycle in unsecured lending that has three or four times the volatility of GDP. Secured lending does have the same 7½-year cycle as GDP. It is possibly out of phase and not closely related to income, suggesting that the findings reported by Aikman et al. (2014) and Goodhart and Hoffman (2008) that credit in the 1985–2006 era did not affect house price inflation are supported. This goes against the case of a pro-cyclical impact of house prices on lending, upon which the financial accelerator is based.

Gordon (2013) notes that when budgets are tighter, the purchase of durables can often be postponed. If so, consumption expenditures on durables would be pro-cyclical. Leamer posits that durables lead the cycle. A common cycle is revealed for both, with CDs leading GDP. This is consistent with consumer durable spending reflecting expected future transitory income growth. It could also cause it through greater employment following the production said durables.

Benito and Wood (2005) see housing and consumer durables to be complementary. Buyers are motivated to 'decorate' the characteristics of their newly purchased property. Alternatively, higher house prices could induce a wealth effect or an equity withdrawal effect (Muellbauer 2007). Unsecured Lending has a close association with house prices at the key cycle of 10 years. It appears that, despite smoothing, NCD are sensitive to both income and house prices at the 10 year cycle. It could be that, rather than equity withdrawal, unsecured lending provides the strong credit link. It appears that, despite smoothing, NCD are sensitive to both income and house prices at the 10-year cycle. It could be that unsecured lending rather than equity withdrawal provides the strong credit link. This may reflect a liberal approach to lending affecting consumption in general, or those overstretched when house purchasing seeking additional borrowing. In a Madsen sense, getting over the first few mortgage payments may be the horizon. Planning any further is unnecessary. Campbell and Cocco (2007) also find a significant relationship between house prices and non-durable consumption growth.

Housing vintages are also considered. *New* house prices are found to be distinctive at a periodicity associated with construction, implying *New* dwellings capture for the builder some capital that would otherwise be transferred from one homeowner to another. Although there is an agreement between Granger causality and phase over *Modern* and *Old*, *New* dwelling leadership is not consistent. Pairwise Granger causality should provide the same inferences as for the phase value, but the latter is only assessed at key cycles. Unlike Granger causality, knowledge of the underlying data generating process or model structure is unnecessary for interpretation of phase diagrams. It could be the Granger result that changes with additional variables in the VAR. Stein's notion of 'fishing' corresponds with speculative building in expectation of future heightened demand. Construction expenditure leads prices. A theme of price anticipation would suggest *New* would lead *Older* house prices.

The received wisdom from OMR, Borgerson, and Sommervoll et al. is that the repeat buyer and first-time buyer are in separate but hierarchically arranged property markets. They model pricing of two types of housing: flats and houses, interlocked by the finance of the two groups with the repeat buyer relying on the first-time buyer to purchase their flat as they buy a house. Granger causality and phase both point to the reverse leadership: the repeat buyer market leads the FTB. Coulson and McMillen (2007) find better lead lesser, worse quality housing. Although not precisely cheap versus expensive or low- versus high-quality housing, the FTB would be buying a cheaper dwelling than a repeat buyer. As such, the finding is consistent with Coulson and McMillen.

Although there are three cycles, the common cycles are consistent with Sommervoll et al.'s house price model. At odds with OMR, FTB price volatility is greater than RBs; fluctuations in the FTB market are not amplified in RB markets; and FTBs do not lead RBs.

7.5 Buyer Groups and the Ripple Effect

The dispersion of house price changes across space, of all the 'ripple' types, has had the most attention. Meen's definition, where a series of regional house price increases are evident in the order identified by the distance from the leading region, is taken as a process that covers the entire UK.

The standard ripple explanations propose a transfer of prices to other regions with only a partial explanation of the mechanism to achieve this. Generally, there is no discussion of price transference across more than two regions. Rather than rely on ad hoc overspill, persistent interactions are considered here based on a balanced and imbalanced economy approaches, which are drawn from work on international regional integration. Moreover, an urban system is discussed, and the urban monocentric urban model is reviewed. The monocentric urban model provides a framework for explaining the co-movement of prices within an area where commuting is viable, extending the boundary of influence, in the case of London, to much of the south-east.

One distinguishing feature in house prices is in the level and extent of regional volatilities. A second is in the order of response. The regions with the greatest volatilities are found in the Midlands, whereas London and the UK reference series have the smallest. Both are consistent with a balanced economy model where the asynchronicity inherent in a ripple reduces the volatility in the UK series (weighted average of the regions). Moreover, London has one of the lower coherence values, more consistent with a ripple/balanced economy than an urban system model.

It was proposed that a ripple in a cycle perspective requires common regional cycles. A 10.67-year cycle is featured in the power spectrum of the largest minority of regions for FTBs, whereas this 6.4-year cycle performs the same function for RBs. This shorter cycle combines regions surrounding Greater London. Three cycles dominate both buyer groups.

The common cycles and the phase results substantiate the cyclical perspective of regional interaction. Phase reveals an ordering in repeat buyers across the UK consistent with a ripple with only a slight misordering in the south-east. The same is broadly true for FTBs. The anomalies are outer metropolitan leading all regions and the north preceding the northern regions.

Urban systems have a hierarchy of nodes. The imprint of the dominant node's cycle should be evident in national perturbations, and responses should be based on the node ordering not distance. As London's series, even with phase adjustment, does not reflect the UK's series as closely as others, and regions with larger centres respond after those with smaller, these results are not consistent with a nodal model.

7.6 Robust Cycles

Finding that RB price leads [and follow] FTB prices is consistent with other 'ripple' work that points to more expensive house prices leading less expensive (Coulson and McMillen 2007; Ho et al. 2008; Hui 2011; Smith and Ho 1996). Diffusion in the greater south-east/Midlands area can be explained by the relatively high price in London and its extensive *commuting* shed in this area. Beyond this, commuting to London cannot explain co-movement.

Finding that expected long-run common trends are not in evidence, given the emphasis on cycles, one could focus on De Groot and Franses' (2008) robust cycles assertion as opposed to a shock perspective. What is found is that cycles in the liberalised era are longer than in the earlier 30 years. The great moderation could have altered the business cycle through changes in consumption and the move towards permanent income-type smoothing (Campbell and Mankiw 1991), shifting the emphasis on the income–consumption link onto longer cycles. That would not change the intensification of the link between consumption and income, but the smoothing would be consistent with the change in an aggregate consumption effect. Secured lending does not appear to be linked closely to consumption and house prices, but unsecured does. This is consistent with Wunder (2012) and the change in business cycle drivers from investment towards consumption and debt. The rise of the credit and store cards would boost and smooth consumption for the financially stretched, such as the FTB, who may be better able to weather current income constraints during the earlier years of house mortgage repayments. The option to resort to secured lending may have high set-up costs but still available if needed.

There are symptoms of a strong wealth effect in the second era which not there in the first period. However, a test of Cutler's assertion that there would be a stronger link between house prices and consumption expenditure in the financially liberalised era is not supported. The test though considers the link across all cycles, so a switch of cycle emphasis would not necessarily render the link more intense.

Another contributory factor to longer cycles is a change in the construction response. With a smaller downward force the cumulative effect of increasing supply would take longer to reach the turning point in the price cycle, heralding an era of larger bubbles and/or longer housing cycles. If the cycle is construction-driven as Leamer suggests, one could see that income, consumption, and price cycles would all 'lengthen'.

Turning to the explanations adapted from spatial diffusion literature that predicts a top-down price transfer, one could suggest prices are driven by expectations. It could be that the more expensive repeat buyer dwellings act as markers, signalling changes in cheaper or lower-quality properties. Taking this forward, expectations models with house prices would have to have some spatial and temporal price overspill: prices are serially dependent locally and are affected by activity in neighbouring areas (Dolde and Tirtiroglu 1997; McDonald 1985; Pollakowski and Ray 1997). This does not require commuting for price transmission; it encompasses [information] overspill and sits within elements of Meen-Wood ripple explanations. In this perspective, Irish and Australian spillover results, where overlapping housing markets cannot be used to explain co-movement, are more intellectually attractive.

Quality tiers are presumed to be overlapping. Repeat buyers may be forced to search in lower quality as sub-market prices become less affordable, affecting those that would appeal to FTBs. Both FTB and RB are subject to banks' credit policies and mortgage rates. A relaxation of credit restrictions does not seem to favour consumption or investment finance; banks are equally incapable of assessing their repayment capacity (Schularick and Taylor 2012). As such, the two buyer groups would exhibit similar dynamics, but the RB is better placed to arrange finance, which could explain their house price leadership. When the price differential is suitably large, trading down from a more expensive/larger to a smaller/cheaper abode, possibly in a different region, is a further avenue for expensive driving cheaper dwellings.

7.7 Policy and Future Research: Recycling and Society

The top-down explanations for diffusion of price among quality tiers do not recognise the potential dislocation of the FTB as price rises, and yet, it appears that FTB and RB participation is linked. With the bottom-up approach, the repeat buyer's house acquisition is funded, in part, through the affordability of the flat. With RB leading FTB, the price codetermination process becomes more opaque. House price increases will stall when flats become unaffordable.

The relationship between the RB and FTB proposed by OMR provides a clear view of finance and suggests how the numbers of buyers are linked. The reverse causation is more problematic, yet this is what is revealed here. Three avenues of recycling funds are discussed. The RB feeds the FTB's need for funding through intergenerational transfers. Combining Borgersen (2014a, b, c), there is a circuit of recycled equity from flat to terrace home to family house and back to flat again. Second, implicitly OMR offer the same circuit through the lifecycle of moves where the downsizing in the third age injects capital from the family house market back into flats. That said, there is evidence that, like bed-blockers, mature households without children, by not moving are affecting the recycling of dwellings, preventing some from moving onto larger houses and consequently vacating smaller ones for FTBs. Local Authority taxes more linked to the size of a dwelling might ease this pressure so that there is a major disincentive for a single person to occupy a four bedroomed house.

Third, there is evidence that FTBs are crowded out by BTL investors. Pryce and Sprigings (2009) buy-to-let proposition predicts greater volatility within the FTB market and an injection of equity into the flat market. BTL mortgages are a recent phenomenon that appears to have created a dislocation in buyer relations. The impact of intergenerational transfers and BTL buyers on house price inflation could be estimated in further research. Also, more work is needed on the role of the FTB and the ripple effect across UK space.

A large number of first-time buyers are not a necessity for the recycling of dwellings and the maintenance of the repeat buyer market. The landlord could facilitate that. Whilst injecting volatility, financial liberalisation and intergenerational financial transfers permit some first-time buyers to keep up with repeat buyers.

Construction has become less price sensitive over the 60 years. The Barker (2003) report highlights vested interests among local authorities, homeowners, and builders in maintaining low construction rates. The planning process is restrictive and insensitive to price signals. DiPasquale and Wheaton's supply side of their pricing model is predicted on construction being stimulated by the higher price.

Construction is one means of deflating a house price bubble. Building needs to be made more price sensitive.

As they are difficult to moderate, particularly when accommodated by the availability of credit, adaptive price expectations may present policy conundrums. When in a bubble period this credit is probably secured against the assets whose prices are inflated by speculation (Spotton 1997). This is complicated by persistent asynchronised regional cycles. If countercyclical monetary policy is geared towards managing house price inflation in the leading region and that is out of phase with the following region, seeking to moderate the cycle amplitude in one will exaggerate the other. This highlights the need for a rules-based, non-interest rate policy for UK house price management. Gregoriou et al. (2014) find that lending is decoupling from earnings. The Bank of England has imposed some limits on lending ratios, which is an appropriate response. It would make sense to focus on income multiples and non-housing equity to moderate financial accelerator-cyclical effects. Capital gains tax could be used more vigorously to temper the speculative investor-buyer. If the equity growth was taxed heavily, the speculative relocation would be much reduced. That notwithstanding, in a Minsky world, the metrics would be temporary, and liberalising forces will undermine these limits eventually as the financier trumps the regulator, providing the basis for a super-cycle.

Overall, the work suggests that without some radical changes to both the supply of dwellings and the mixture of buyers at the bottom end of the market, the average age of the first-time buyer will rise. A key implication is that the buy-to-let buyer may be supporting repeat buyer prices whilst excluding many from poorer backgrounds from house purchase permanently, contributing to both financial and social instabilities. Recent changes to the taxing of buy-to-let properties are making it more difficult for the landlord to make property renting pay, but these need to be more vigorous.

London's cycle does not turn out to be relatively volatile. The focus should be its price trend. The Bank of England has imposed some limits on lending ratios but not on repayment periods. The duration of a repayment mortgage is drifting from 25 to 35 years (Giles 2016), with a quarter of first-time buyers taking out a 35-year mortgage in 2015 facilitating this. The Bank of England is worried by the implications of repayment period extending into retirement. Thus, the mortgage lending cycle could be extended in the same way as other cycles in the liberalised era, spreading purchasing over a longer, perhaps dangerous horizon. This is an oversight that needs addressing before it becomes the norm.

References

Aikman, D., Haldane, A., & Nelson, B. (2014). Curbing the credit cycle. *The Economic Journal, 125*(June), 1072–1109.

Attanasio, O., Leicester, A., & Wakefield, M. (2011). Do house prices drive consumption growth? The coincident cycles of house prices and consumption in the UK. *Journal of the European Economic Association, 9*(3), 399–435.

Barker, K. (2003). *Review of Housing Supply: Interim Report–Analysis*. London: HMSO.

Benito, A., & Wood, R. (2005). How important is housing market activity for durables spending? *Bank of England Quarterly Bulletin,* 45(2), 153–159. Summer.

Borgersen, T.-A. (2014a). Housing careers, house price dispersion and the housing market multiplier. *Housing, Theory and Society, 31*(1), 91–118.

Borgersen, T.-A. (2014b). Equity induced up-trading and the housing market structure. *International Journal of Housing Markets and Analysis, 7*(2), 204–217.

Borgersen, T.-A. (2014c). Heterogeneous housing markets: Structural implications for pricing and risk. *International Journal of Housing Markets and Analysis, 7*(3), 383–396.

Campbell, J., & Cocco, J. (2007). How do house prices affect consumption? *Evidence from Micro Data, Journal of Monetary Economics, 54*(3), 591–621.

Campbell, J., & Mankiw, N. G. (1991). The response of consumption to income: A cross-country investigation. *European Economic Review, 35*(4), 723–756.

Cogley, T., & Nason, J. (1995). Effects of the Hodrick-Pescott filter on trend and difference stationary time series: Implications for business cycle research. *Journal of Economic Dynamics and Control, 19,* 253–278.

Coulson, N., & McMillen, D. (2007). The dynamics of intraurban quantile house price indexes. *Urban Studies, 44*(8), 1517–1537.

Croux, C., Forni, M., & Reichlin, L. (2001). A measure of comovement for economic variables: Theory and empirics. *Review of Economics and Statistics, 83,* 232–241.

Cutler, J. (1995). The housing market and the economy. *Bank of England Quarterly Bulletin,* August, 260–269.

De Groot, B., & Franses, P. (2008). Stability though cycles. *Technological Forecasting and Social Change, 75,* 301–311.

Dolde, W., & Tirtiroglu, D. (1997). Temporal and spatial information diffusion in real estate price changes and variances. *Real Estate Economics, 25*(4), 539–565.

Giles, C. (2016, January 10). 35-year mortgages become the norm, Halifax figures show. http://www.FT.com.

Goodhart, C., & Hofmann, B. (2008). House prices, money, credit, and the macroeconomy. *Oxford Review of Economic Policy, 24*(1), 180–205.

Gordon, R. (2013). *Macroeconomics* (12th ed.). New York: Prentice Hall.

Gregoriou, A., Kontonikas, A., & Montagnoli, A. (2014). Aggregate and regional house price to earnings ratio dynamics in the UK. *Urban Studies, 51*(13) 2916–2927.

Guay, A., & St-Amant, P. (2005). Do the Hodrick-Pescott and Baxter King filters provide a good approximation of business cycles? *Annales D'Economie et de Statistique, 77,* 133–155.

Harvey, A., & Trimbur, T. (2008). Trend estimation and the Hodrick-Prescott filter. *Journal of the Japan Statistical Society, 38*(1), 41–49.

Ho, L., Ma, Y., & Haurin, D. (2008). House price changes across quality tiers. *Journal of Real Estate Finance & Economics, 37*(4), 299–316.

Hui, H.-C. (2011). Cycles in landed and non-landed housing sub-markets in Malaysia. *International Journal of Housing Markets and Analysis, 4*(2), 144–154.

Leamer, E. (2007). *Housing is the business cycle* (Working Paper 13428), NBER.

Leamer, E. (2015). Housing is the business cycle: What survives the lessons of 2008–2009? *Journal of Money Credit and Banking, 47*(1), 43–50.

McDonald, J. (1985). Expectations and urban housing prices. *Urban Studies, 22,* 543–549.

Muellbauer, J. (2007). Housing, credit and consumer expenditure. In *Proceedings-Economic Policy Symposium-Jackson Hole* (pp. 267–334). Kansas City: Federal Reserve Bank of Kansas City.

Phillips, P. C. B., & Jin, S. (2015). *Business cycles, trend elimination, and the HP filter* (Cowles Foundation Discussion Paper No. 2005). New Haven: Yale University.

Pollakowski, H., & Ray, T. (1997). Housing price diffusion patterns at different aggregation levels: An examination of housing market efficiency. *Journal of Housing Research, 8*(1), 107–124.

Pryce, G., & Sprigings, N. (2009). Outlook for UK housing and the implications for policy: Are we reaping what we have sown? *International Journal of Housing Markets and Analysis, 2*(2), 145–166.

Schularick, M., & Taylor, A. (2012). Credit booms gone bust: Monetary policy, leverage cycles, and financial crises, 1870–2008. *American Economic Review, 102*(2), 1029–1061.

Smith, L., & Ho, M. (1996). The relative price differential between higher and lower priced homes. *Journal of Housing Economics, 5,* 1–17.

Sommervoll, D., Borgersen, T.-A., & Wennemo, T. (2010). Endogenous housing market cycles. *Journal of Banking & Finance, 34*(3), 557–567.

Spotton, B. (1997). Financial instability reconsidered: Orthodox theories verses historical facts. *Journal of Economic Literature, 31,* 175–195.

Wunder, T. (2012). Income distribution and consumption driven growth: How consumption behaviors of the top two income quintiles help to explain the economy. *Journal of Economic Issues, 46*(1), 173–192.

Index

D. Gray, *Cycles in the UK Housing Economy*,
DOI 10.1007/978-3-319-63348-0

V

W

Y

The manufacturer's authorised representative in the EU is Springer Nature Customer Service Centre GmbH, Europaplatz 3, 69115 Heidelberg, Germany. If you have any concerns regarding our products, please contact ProductSafety@springernature.com

Printed and bound by CPI Group (UK) Ltd, Croydon, CR0 4YY
25/09/2026
02222890-0003